Integrating the Literature of Chris Van Allsburg in the Classroom

D0406207

by
Thomas J. Palumbo

illustrated by Vanessa Filkins

Cover by Vanessa Filkins

Good Apple
1204 Buchanan St., Box 299
Carthage, IL 62321-0299

SIMON & SCHUSTER *A Paramount Communications Company*

ISBN No. 0-86653-658-2

Printing No. 98765432

Good Apple
1204 Buchanan St., Box 299
Carthage, IL 62321-0299

Table of Contents

Introducing Chris Van Allsburg

What Makes a Successful Author and Illustrator?

Integrating the Literature of Chris Van Allsburg in the Classroom is the third of a five-part series focusing on the most read contemporary authors and illustrators. Like the books before it, *Integrating the Literature of Judy Blume in the Classroom* and *Integrating the Literature of Beverly Cleary in the Classroom*, this book uses the eleven-step format necessary for developing and maximizing the educational benefits of literature used in the classroom or home. Each of the eleven steps is multilevel and can be read to or by children when doing each activity. The activities are not etched in stone. You don't have to use them all. Use the questions and ideas that fit your educational goals and objectives. After you blend your curriculum guide's ideas and your own ideas and the ideas in this series, you will find very few gaps in your literature and language arts program.

About the Author

Chris Van Allsburg's stories and illustrations have fascinated millions of children all over the world. Each new book has an anxious line of teachers and children waiting for it. We ask ourselves "What creative idea or picture is he going to catch our imagination with this time?" Through the creativity of his stories and his award-winning drawings, he has taken us from the gardens of Abdul Gasazi to the hidden dreams of little Ben. Through the magic of his illustrations, we see that his color and black and white pictures are worth more than a thousand words.

Questions You Might Want to Ask Before Using This Guide

1. At what age did Chris Van Allsburg discover his drawing and writing talents? Were they discovered at the same time, or did they develop separately?

2. Chris Van Allsburg does not write of everyday experiences like Judy Blume and Beverly Cleary. Why has this attracted us to his writing and drawings?

3. How did his childhood affect the strange way he makes us look at things? Did he have someone that helped him to see how unique his ideas were?

4. Where does he get the ideas for his stories? Are other authors and illustrators an influence in his work?

5. Where can we go to get some solid inside information about his work and childhood?

6. What other authors would you compare to him? How did you make this determination?

Opening Thoughts and Questions

What makes a good writer, artist, illustrator and author? Why do so many children look forward to seeing Chris Van Allsburg's drawings, as well as hearing/reading his stories? Do you think Chris Van Allsburg's ability to write and draw is an advantage over his contemporaries? You'll get a chance to present your opinions and views on modern writers/illustrators in the "What Is Your Opinion" section throughout this activity book. Try to write your ideas using a variety of sentence structures. Spend some time thinking about your answers before writing them down. Consider how views that are opposite of yours might be expressed. Discuss your ideas with a classmate before writing them. Use the back of your paper if you need to express your ideas more fully.

1. Who are your three favorite authors? What do you like best about them as a group? ______

2. How many Chris Van Allsburg books have you read? Which one is your favorite? Why? ______

3. In learning what makes a good book, do you think it is necessary to read a variety of books by different authors and illustrators? Why? Why not? Please explain. ______

4. Many writers present mysteries/unanswered questions/problems in their stories. By the end of the story the problem is usually solved for better or worse. In many of Chris Van Allsburg's stories, he leaves you hanging without a definite solution to an idea presented in one of his pictures or in his story. Which technique do you prefer? Why? ______

5. Many people talk about the illustrations in Chris Van Allsburg's books. Can you name two of his books and two books of others where the illustrations received as much acclaim as the story? ______

6. What are three things you would like to know about Chris Van Allsburg before beginning this literature activity book? ______

7. Do you think good books, good writing and art techniques should be taught together or separately? Why? Why not? ______

8. Can older children enjoy good artwork as much as younger children? Explain. ______

What Snake? The Lost City

Jumanji

Lost Our Guide

Read the Directions

Keep the House Clean

Game Day Troubles

Monkey Mania Rhino Rundown

Lead-Ins to Literature

Do you believe in the supernatural or witchcraft? Do you think that your dolls and models could come to life? Do you think the events in your favorite board game could suddenly become the events in your life? Do you think the unstoppable can't be stopped? Well, fasten your seat belts, mystery fans! After reading *Jumanji*, you'll be very careful where you store your games and figurines, and you won't make fun of anyone who believes in magic and witchcraft.

1. In the literature that you have read, what are your favorite spells, witches' tricks or unsolved mysteries?

2. If you could pick a game that you would actually see brought to life or could actually enter the game as a human participant, what game would that be? Why?

3. Would you feel more comfortable being cast into a game, if your brother or sister were along? Why or why not?

4. What supplies would you carry with you, if you were thrust into Monopoly, Dungeons and Dragons or your favorite game?

5. What three things do parents always tell children before the children are left home alone?

6. If you found a place of magic and spells, would you tell a friend about it or keep the secret to yourself? Please explain why you would or would not share this place with a friend? Can you give two instances where you would and two where you would not share your secret?

7. The movie *Home Alone* is about a family that goes on vacation and forgets one of their children at home. The child then has to defend the house against robbers. In *Jumanji*, the kids have to defend the house against the events in a game. What game events would you predict a creative author would use to attack a house and its child inhabitants?

8. Where do you think an author would get the idea of bringing a child's game to life?

9. Why do you think the author would pick such a strange title as *Jumanji* for his story? What was the first thing that came to mind when you heard the title?

10. A brother and sister are defending the house. Do you think they will work well together or just get into each other's way?

Just the Facts

1. Where are the parents going on their evening away from home? ________________
2. What kind of game is Jumanji? ________________
3. The directions next to the letter *D* start with what words? ________________
4. The lion roared so loud that it knocked Peter off of his ________________.
5. What number could Judy roll that would cause a second lion to appear in the house? ______
6. How many monkeys were tearing the kitchen apart? ________________
7. What are monsoons? ________________
8. The rain stopped when the ________________ got lost.
9. Who crushed the living room furniture? ________________
10. What caused Judy to shriek and jump on a chair? ________________
11. What was the python wrapped around? ________________
12. Who did the guide sit with on the couch? ________________
13. Molten lava usually comes from a volcano. In *Jumanji,* however, the lava poured out of the ________________.
14. What word seemed to restore everything to order? ________________
15. Where did the kids drop the game after everything in their house went back to normal? ________________.
16. ____________ ____________ had a long, thin box under his arm.
17. What kind of sickness did Mother jokingly think that Peter and Judy had? ________________
18. What did Mrs. Budwing bring the children? ________________
19. Daniel and Walter never finish ________________.
20. Daniel and Walter don't read ________________.
21. What do you lose when a guide is lost? ________________

What Is Your Opinion?

1. What age would you "guesstimate" the children were if they were old enough to be alone?

2. Did you think it was funny that the parents never gave the children any emergency numbers or other helpful hints other than "keep the house neat"?

3. What do you think was on Judy and Peter's mind when they giggled with delight after their parents left?

4. When you are bored, are there more things inside your house or outside your house that will keep your attention?

5. If there were a lion in your house, don't you think you would get out of the house immediately? Explain please.

6. Why do you think people hide under their beds? Certainly, everyone knows that fact and will look under the bed first.

7. Which event would you estimate caused the most damage to the house? Why?

8. Were the kids in another dimension from the guide and that is why he could not hear them, or was there another reason for his deafness to them?

9. Each event did more destruction to the house. Why do you think the kids assumed everything would be okay after the game was over? Nothing in the directions said this situation would right itself at the game's conclusion.

10. How does the eight-foot length of the python in the story compare to the world's largest pythons?

11. What other move on the gameboard would you have added to cause greater havoc in the house?

12. Would you have warned the Budwing children about the game they had under their arms before they took it into their house and destroyed the decor?

13. Of the award-winning illustrations in *Jumanji*, which one was your favorite? Why?

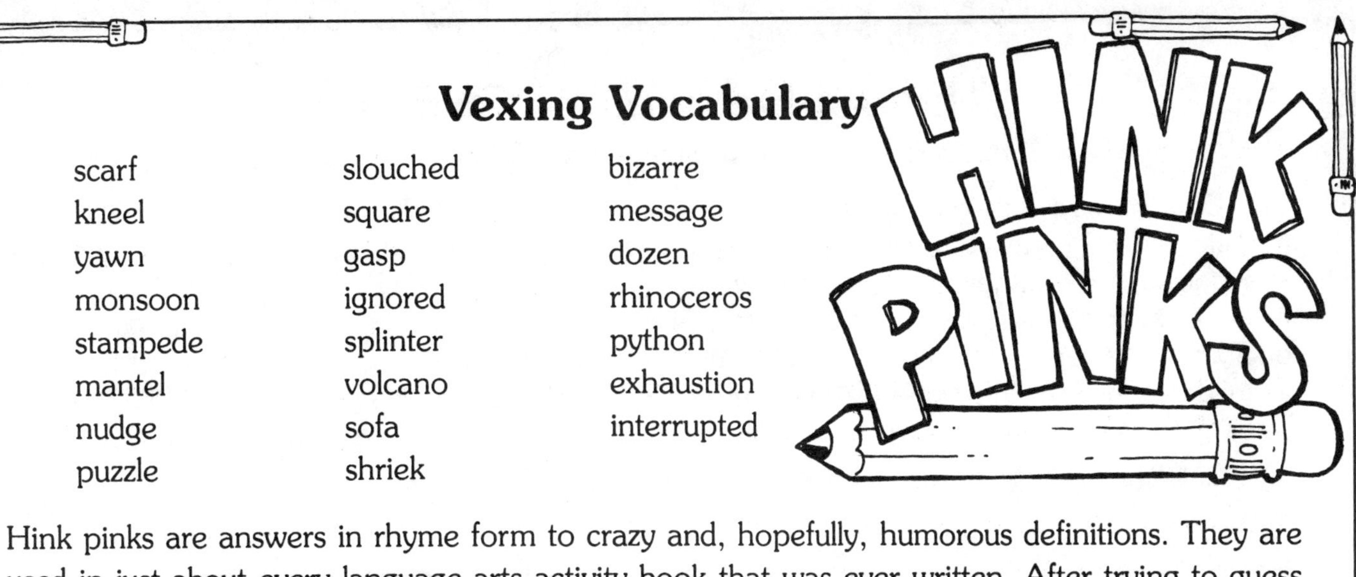

Vexing Vocabulary

scarf	slouched	bizarre
kneel	square	message
yawn	gasp	dozen
monsoon	ignored	rhinoceros
stampede	splinter	python
mantel	volcano	exhaustion
nudge	sofa	interrupted
puzzle	shriek	

Hink pinks are answers in rhyme form to crazy and, hopefully, humorous definitions. They are used in just about every language arts activity book that was ever written. After trying to guess the hink pinks that will satisfy the clues below, can you incorporate your vocabulary list or another list in this book into hink pink questions/answers?

1. How does a mother deer know that her youngster is tired? ______________________________

2. What would hundred-leg insects running wild be called? ______________________________

3. If your mother's brothers and sisters have loads of children, you probably have ______________________________.

4. If you had a wood piece stuck in your hand during a snowstorm, it could be called a ______________________________.

5. What would an exploding can of cleaner that usually unclogs your sink pipes be called? ______________________________

6. A mild scream might be a ______________________________.

7. Children with nothing to do that no one pays attention to might be called the ______________________________.

8. A twelve o'clock rain in Japan is called a ______________________________.

9. A weird running automobile is a ______________________________.

10. A missing snake might be called a ______________________________.

11. A poorly drawn rectangular figure is a ______________________________.

12. The unsolved mystery of the dog that would not stop biting people was called a ______________________________.

Try writing definitions for these answers: funny bunny, big wig, damp tramp, red bed, whale's tales, pink drink, jolly collie, merry cherry, astute fruit, glad dad, heavy Chevy, core store, pleasant pheasant.

The Double Acrostic Challenge
Drills for Skills

The Double Acrostic Challenge will stimulate your vocabulary and critical thinking skills. Each acrostic should be filled in with words going across. The object is that by critical planning you also can create another word going down. If I start with "C . . A . . T" written down, I then have to think of three words of three letters each. One must begin with *C*, one with *A* and one with *T*. After I write my three selections across, I check to see if another word has been formed downward. With good planning, more than one word can be created down. This activity leads to making magic squares where words are formed in every direction. Score five points for every word you make down. Place your score on the blank next to each grid.

Example:

Ideas and Illustrations

The book *Jumanji* revolves around a board game of the same name. Once the game was begun, the game and all its weird consequences could not be stopped until the final destination was reached and the winner yelled "Jumanji." You'll remember the monkeys, snake, rhinoceros, lion and lost hunter from your readings. What other features do you think the game had that weren't landed on and discussed in the story? Eight boxes are provided for you below. Each box is representative of one square on the Jumanji gameboard. Design that box the way it would look if it were a part of the original board game. Place the most creative of your eight drawings/box designs on an 8" x 8" (20.32 x 20.32 cm) piece of paper. Place your classmates' best works next to yours on a wall. Make the wall look like a giant board game with each of the boxes selected. This is the same approach that is used in an old-time quilting bee. Everyone makes one square for a quilt. Each square is sewn together with other squares to form a quilt. Discuss other gameboard favorites with your classmates. Your teacher may want you to pick your favorite board game, say Monopoly, and design eight additional boxes that could be part of the game you selected.

Short-Term Project I

A time machine and magical letter have transported you back to the time of Charlemagne (740-814), King of the Franks. Charlemagne has summoned you to his court. The monk, Einhard, wrote the letter, but you recognized the cross and krls of the king at the bottom. The king probably wants you to replace Count Hruodland, leader of his rear guard. The Muslim Saracens killed Hruodland at Roncesvalles, and the king has not been able to find someone strong and brave enough to assume this responsibility. You read about Hruodland's bravery and heroics centuries later, thanks to the epic poem *The Song of Roland*. You understand the importance Charlemagne placed on his friendship with Hruodland. To your surprise Charlemagne doesn't want you to serve in his army, but wants you to go back to the future and design a gameboard like Jumanji's that will teach children about Charlemagne and his time. He suggests that the game include some of his famous battles and conquests. Charlemagne expects you to return in two weeks to present your game plans to the court. Design your game after answering the questions below. Your teacher may want you to design a gameboard chronicling Lee, Grant, Alexander the Great, Martin Luther King, Harriet Tubman, Julius Caesar or some other historical figure.

1. What is the name of your board game? ______________________

____

2. What two sources did you use in your research? ______________________

____

3. What will be a key outcome in playing your game? ______________________

____

4. Describe four historical facts that your board will portray. ______________________

____

____

5. How can your game be won? ______________________

____

6. What will be the cost of your game and what type of pieces will be needed to play your game? ______________________

____

7. What age level will your game be designed to reach? How could you make your game so it will appeal to many different age groups? ______________________

____

Draw a copy of your game on the back of this sheet.

Book Review Form

Short-Term Project II

Children in my classroom often ask how our textbooks were chosen. I explain to them that most school districts have a textbook review committee. The committee is composed of teachers, parents, supervisors, school administrators and sometimes students. The committee is responsible for evaluating textbooks and other educational materials. They usually have a book review form that assists them in evaluating those materials placed before their committee. The books that receive the best evaluation scores are usually selected for use in that particular district. However, cost is also a consideration. Below you will find a form similar to those used throughout the country with additional questions pertaining to the books used in this resource book on Chris Van Allsburg's writings. Pick three of Chris Van Allsburg's books or one book from each of three authors to evaluate with this form. Try to place a numerical value on each question and determine what a good evaluation total should be. Add three additional questions at the bottom of this page which you think should be included in this survey.

1. What is the name of the book or text you are evaluating? ____________________
2. Who is/are the author(s)? ____________________
3. What company publishes this book? ____________________
4. How much does one book cost?____________________ Classroom set?__________

Use a scale of 1-10 (poor-excellent) for these questions.

5. Is the cover attractive and motivating? ____________________
6. Are minority or ethnic characters part of the story? ____________________
7. Are minority or ethnic characters used in the illustrations? ____________________
8. Does the book correspond to our curriculum? ____________________
9. Are the directions clear and easy to follow? ____________________
10. Were the characters well developed? ____________________
11. Was the plot easy to follow and believable? ____________________
12. Did the author give good descriptions of the various settings in both words and pictures?
    ____

Please use the back of this form to answer these questions with a statement.

13. Did the book change your ideas or feelings in any way?
14. Was the book informational?
15. What were the books strongest features? Weakest?
16. Give a brief statement as to why this book should or shouldn't be selected by this committee.
17. If you think this book shouldn't be selected by this committee, what helpful hints would you recommend to the company for their book's/story's/product's improvement?
18. Brief book description to be placed in our guide.

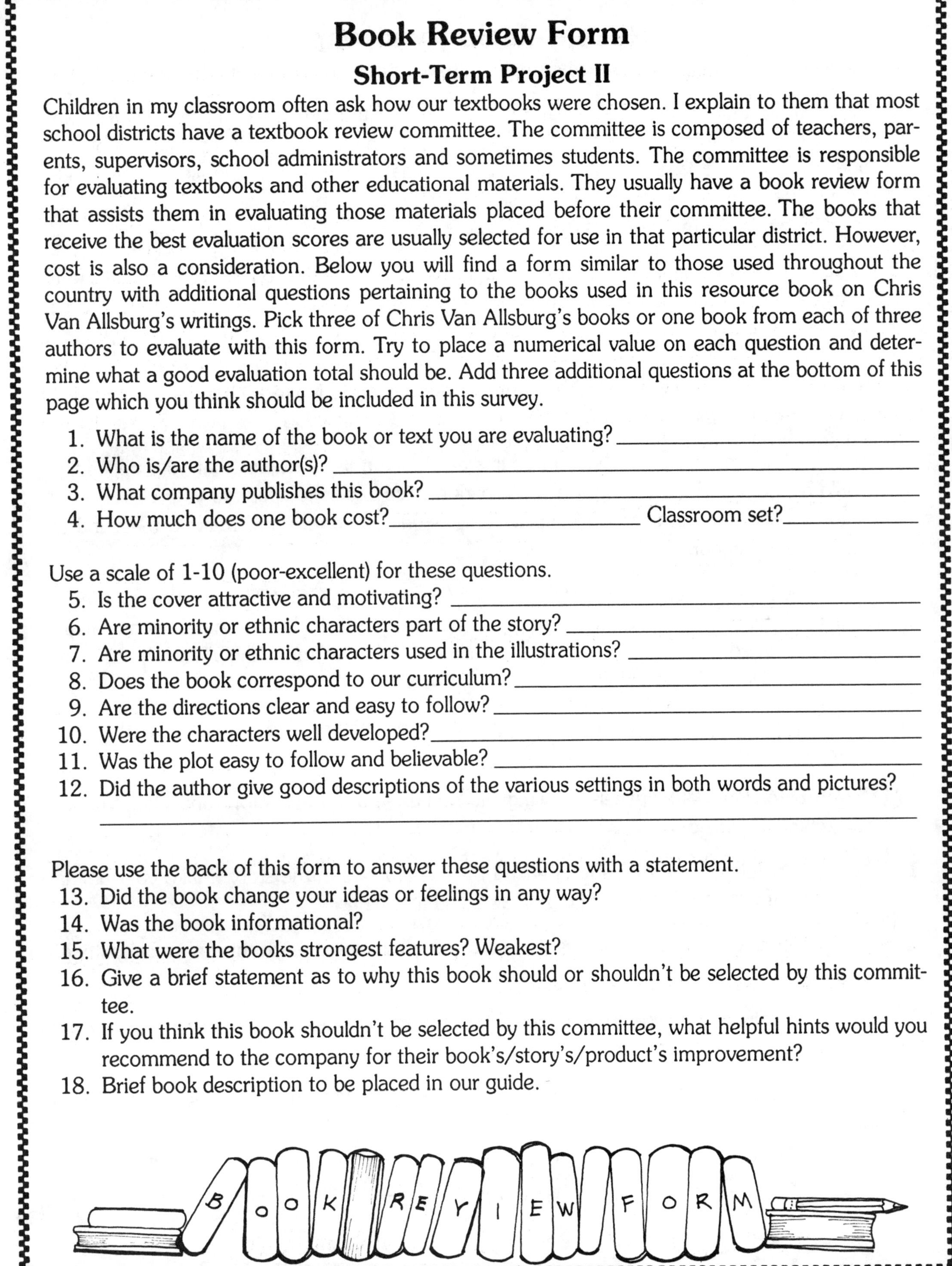

Research Suggestions

1. Make a drawing or mural of animals that you would not want to meet in *Jumanji*.
2. When studying endangered species, you will find that the pet trade and the killing of animals because of the erroneous beliefs concerning the mythical, mystical properties of their body parts, take a large toll of many animal populations. Research the illegal uses of elephant tusks, rhino horns, animal furs/skins, gorilla hands, etc. What strategies would you employ to prevent the senseless destruction of thousands of animals?
3. Write to a local or national conservation agency for information on topics from wildlife to forests.
4. Make a survey in your classroom of the top ten board games that your classmates play.
5. Research three types of child care programs in your area. Make a chart comparing daily fees, weekly and monthly rates.
6. What national parks do you have in your area? Make a list of topics that your classmates would be interested in studying. Recruit a park service expert to speak to your class on one of the topics. Plan an imaginary trip to Yellowstone National Park. Make a map and an itinerary for the journey.
7. Write a guidebook that children can use when they are lost. Call it *The Survival Guide for Lost Children*. Remember to list important numbers in it. Include some jokes and funny things to do, so they don't cry when they are lost. Include "must know" information and pictures for kids that can't read.
8. Pick another game to insert in the story instead of Jumanji and explain how the story would be different.
9. Design before and after panels showing the scenes in *Jumanji* before and after the animals/guide got loose/lost.
10. Pick classmates to play the parts of each of the characters in the story. Make your animal props out of papier-mâché. Stuffed animals could also be used.
11. Write another series of happenings that could be added to an "Adventures in Babysitting" story.
12. Design an animal crossword puzzle. See if you can make a design before searching for the answers that will fit your design.
13. Design a judging sheet that can be used to rate the illustrations in *Jumanji* and other books that you have read.

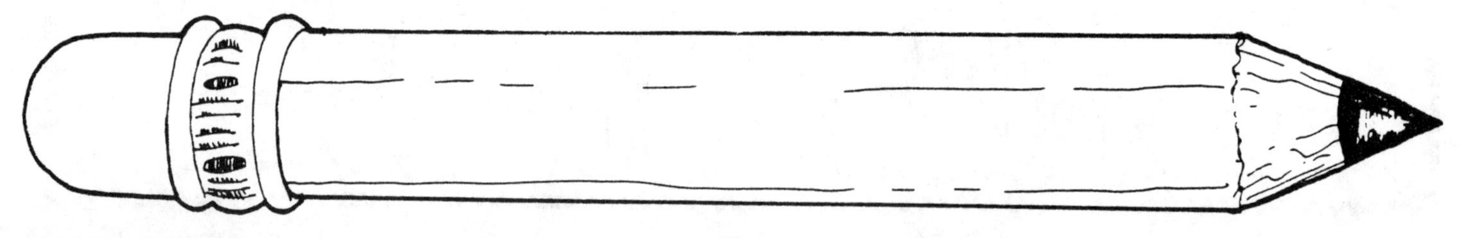

Teacher Suggestions

1. Have your students design posters with the theme "If one of my games could come to life, I would want it to be...." Ask your students to illustrate the unique features of the game and to highlight the reasons for their game choice.

2. The film *Donald in Mathmagicland* is an excellent teaching tool for mathematics, art, history and music instruction. The segment related to *Jumanji* involves Donald being thrust into the middle of a chess game that seems to be coming to life. This might be a good lead-in for the *Jumanji* story.

3. Research with your class the process of registering a painting, board game or written work. How is each process different?

4. The Cover-to-Cover Series on most educational TV stations is excellent. An artist introduces stories by drawing pictures as he tries to motivate children into reading the books that he introduces on each show. In Philadelphia, we store the tapes in a central bank. You send a blank tape in and the ten stories or readings that you are covering in your curriculum are copied for you. They, then, can be shown as part of your daily lessons. With a good pause frame, the children love drawing along with the artist as he introduces each story.

5. Have the class investigate "game packaging." Have each student bring in the box (not the game) that houses his/her favorite game. You can talk about how we would classify the packaging before you talk about the specific features that might attract us to buy the game displayed. Have your students evaluate whether the age recommendations on the packaging are correct. Are the pieces easily replaceable and worth the price of the game? Who holds the game patent? How durable is the game and packaging?

6. Have each child design a game. The assignment can be open-ended or centered around a particular subject area. For example, each child would have to pick a country and then design a game with the theme "Lost Safari to ________________." Remind the class that educational facts must be interspersed in their game procedures.

7. Make a price range questionnaire with your class. It could be as simple as what price range would you pay for a game . . . car . . . book . . . movie . . . lunch . . . dinner . . . computer . . . TV, or you can make your questionnaire more sophisticated by having prices included that people would circle. Have each child give the survey to an adult and a child; then compile and evaluate your questionnaire. What conclusions can be made?

8. How do game makers use the five aspects of creativity?

Write Like a Master

The theme for these story starters is that something has come to life that you didn't expect to be animated or that you have been thrust into the middle of a game or situation in which humans normally don't appear. Try to visualize yourself in each situation and write, trying predictable and unpredictable formats for each story starter.

Story Starter I

Listen, Alice! Wonderland is a great place, but Mom's dinner is at six and I'm tired of eating mushrooms, cookies, tea and tarts. Stop crying! I tried to help you with your problems. You have to realize that no one in the last hundred years has been able to help you. Why do you think that I ______________________________

Story Starter II

If he/she throws me off that wall one more time, I'll . . . I'll. Why do people buy things without reading the labels? It says "tennis ball" not "wall ball." My headache won't go away this way. I miss the clay and grass of the tennis courts. Maybe I should say something to my new owner. He/She will be knocked off his/her seat when English starts coming from my mouth. Maybe I should use my German or French instead. No, I'll try to ______________________________

Story Starter III

The most boring life in the world is the life of a checker. All we do is slide and jump. Even getting kinged isn't ______________________________

Story Starter IV

The magic of my radio is that the listener is transported into the song that is playing. Sometimes this is neat and at other times . . . hold on . . . I'll show you. Here comes a song (whisk people into your favorite song while completing this idea). ______________________________

Gameboard

Materials Needed: Two number cubes, movers, light-colored crayons; Vexing Vocabulary; Just the Facts; student-made and teacher-made question cards can be placed in the areas provided for them in the center of the gameboard. They are optional but highly recommended. A card is picked each time a player has a multiple of five points in his/her bank (5, 10, 15, 20, or 25).

Players Needed: Two to four players or teams of two players

Play Procedures: Players alternate turns; throw number cubes; move in either direction at any time. This allows for playing strategies, rather than just mindlessly moving around a gameboard.

The Roll: Roll both number cubes. Your teacher will tell you to conduct some math operation with the number cubes. The three rules used most often in my classroom are

(a) Subtract the smaller from the larger; then move that many spaces (6 - 4 =2). Move two spaces.

(b) Multiply the two cubes and move the number of spaces in the one's column of the answer (2 x 6 = 12). Move two spaces.

(c) Keep on adding the two cubes until you get one digit as the answer (6 + 6 = 12, 12 = 1 + 2 = 3). Move three spaces. Mathematicians call this finding the digital root.

Object: To score twenty-five points or to capture four cries for help, games or endangered animals. Owning cries, games and animals can be accomplished by landing on them in a normal turn, trading for them when you land on a trading post or buying one of them for two times their value when you land on the bank. Each time you land on a property you color in (or initial) the little block in the corner of the property and put the points in your running bank. Ownership will change after trades. Cross them out on the score sheet and add them to the other column. A scoreboard is provided for you. Each time someone lands on your property, he must pay you the number of points indicated in the top right-hand corner. Each time you land on your own property, you receive twice the points shown.

Winning Sets: Games (Monopoly, bingo, checkers and chess); cries (Save me, We're lost, SOS and Mayday); endangered animals (koala bear, panda, gorilla and black-footed ferret)

Player One's Properties/Score	Player Two's Properties/Score

Game Card Property Pieces

On this page are the twelve game pieces for *Jumanji*. Cut them out and place them on oaktag to prolong their usability. Place a little box next to the gameboard as a storage area. Each time someone lands on an appropriate board space, he receives points and one of the game cards to verify property ownership. It also makes property trading much easier. The next time you play the game, design your own game card property pieces. Design a gameboard and create your own educational board game. Pick a theme. Then try to add important facts and intellectual flavor to your game.

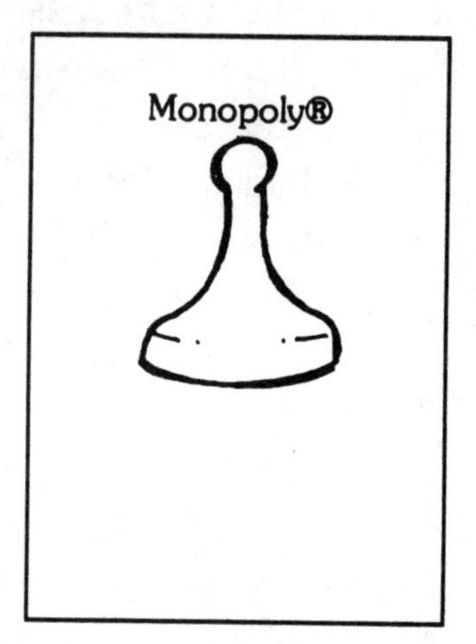

B	I	N	G	O
1	25	3	9	11
16	27	9	2	9
26	24		22	14
13	7	15	2	17
18	20	10	21	23

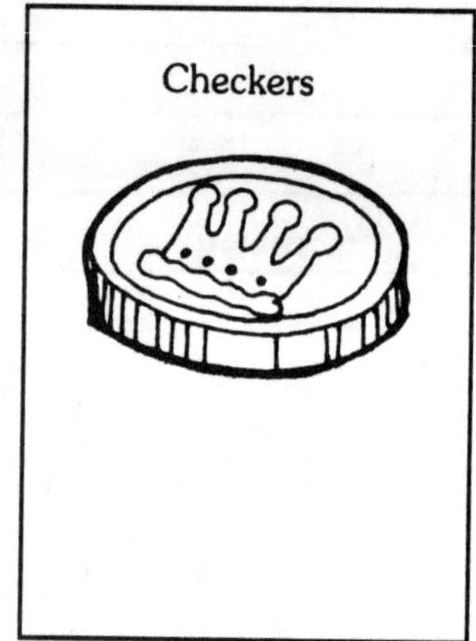

From Games to Gorillas

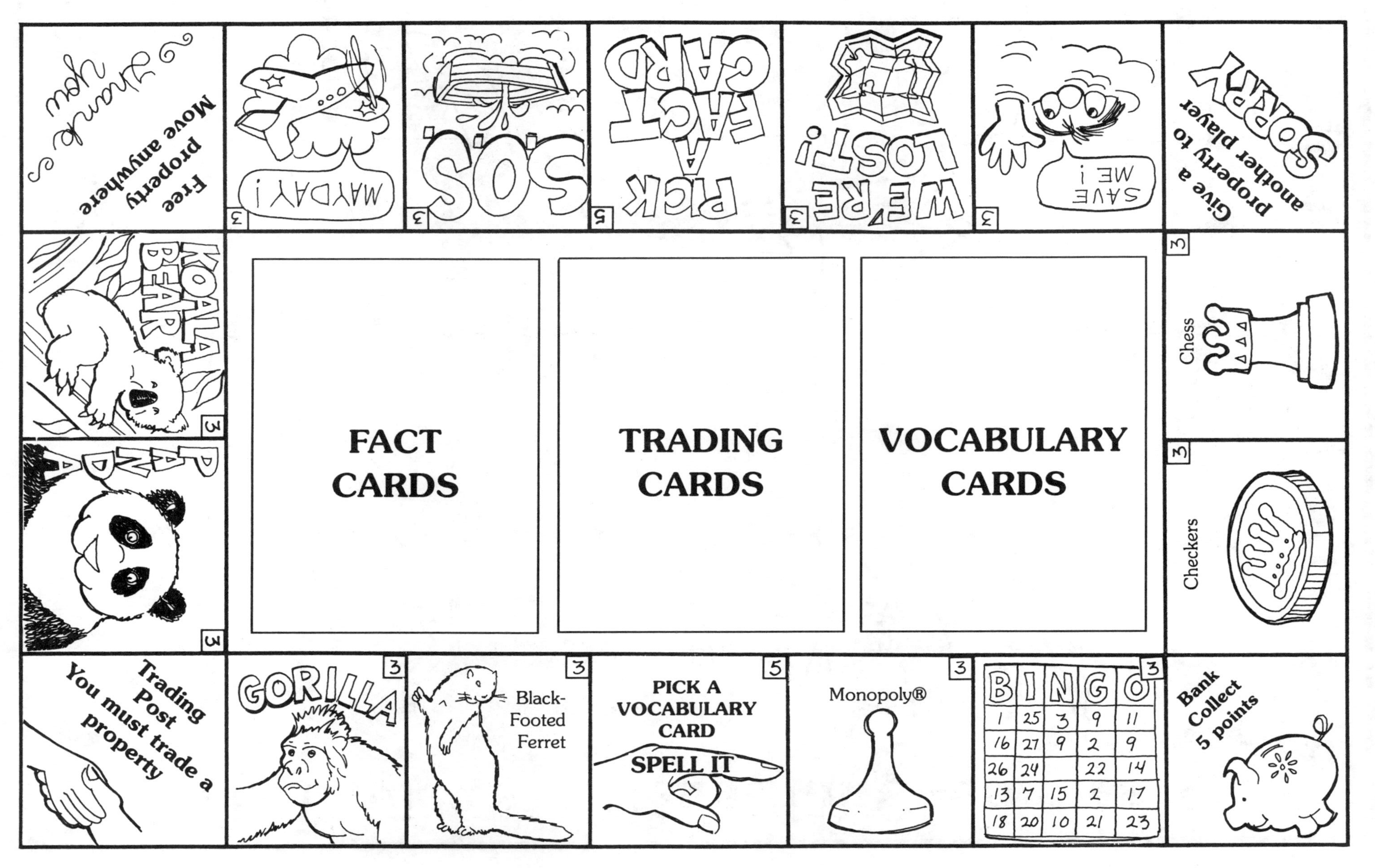

Stage Fright

Curtain Call

The Z Was Zapped

Beautiful Costumes

Great Acting

Flying

Lost

Washing

Running

Good Lighting

Tumbling

Jumping

Frying

Mystery

Hidden Clues

Lead-Ins to Literature

The Zapped Z? I didn't have a clue what the book was about until I read the cover page. It is a play. It sounds like a long play. It has twenty-six acts. You will definitely enjoy the play, if you appreciate humor. Mystery fans will also be challenged by many of the acts. The real challenge comes after reading the play. Can you think of other parts each of the lead characters can play?

1. How much time do you feel you will need to read a twenty-six-act play? When will you do the reading? ______________________________

____

2. Can you think of three topics that will keep school-aged children's attention through twenty-six acts? ______________________________

____

3. If you took a survey of the children in your class, do you think more students would enjoy a comedy or a mystery? ______________________________

____

4. List three plays that you have read. Are there any plays that you are familiar with but haven't read? ______________________________

____

5. How many characters and backstage people would you predict are necessary to create a twenty-six-act play? ______________________________

____

6. Can you find three facts about Chris Van Allsburg's life that will give you clues about *The Z Was Zapped* themes? List your findings. ______________________________

____

7. Try to predict what *zapped* means. List your three best guesses. ______________________________

____

8. What kind of theater would be available in your school or community to house this play? Pick two locations that would be suitable for this production. ______________________________

____

____

9. If you were a member of a production company, what three jobs would you be qualified to do? ______________________________

____

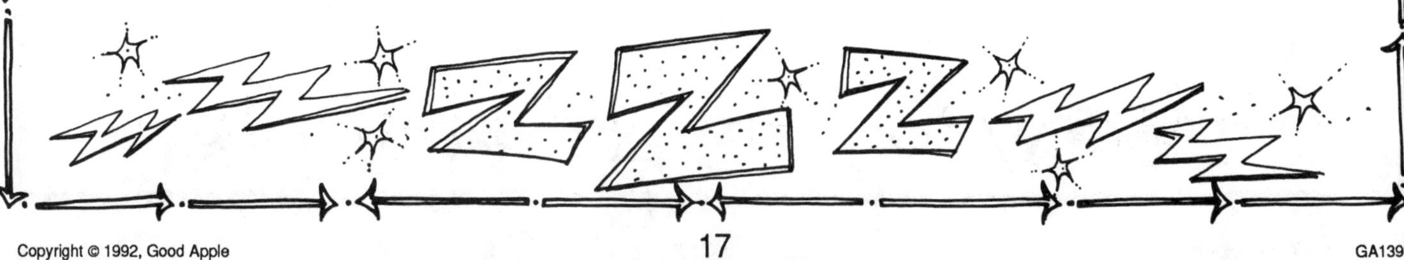

Just the Facts

1. How many parts was the Z broken into and what hit it? ____________________
2. What yanked the Y? ____________________
3. Which section of the V was vanishing? ____________________
4. What appeared in the X-rayed part of the letter? ____________________
5. Who is the cue card holder? ____________________
6. What bit the B? ____________________
7. Where did the I's icing come from? ____________________
8. What problem did the L have? ____________________
9. What three facts can you list concerning the letter Q? ____________________

   a. ____________________

   b. ____________________

   c. ____________________
10. What covered the O? ____________________
11. What two things might have made the J jittery? ____________________

    ____

    ____
12. What letter was covered by a cloth? What design did the letter's cloth cover have? ____________________

    ____
13. How many creatures had parts in the play, and who were they? ____________________

    ____
14. What three things could the M have been made of to cause it to melt? ____________________

    ____

    ____
15. What damaged the N? ____________________

What Is Your Opinion?

1. What three acts were your favorites? Explain, please. ______________________________

2. Of the twenty-six acts, which two were the least creative? Please explain the reasons for your choices. ______________________________

3. What would you suggest to the alphabet theater for their next production? To whom would your selected topic appeal? ______________________________

4. Do you feel that extra training would be needed for the actors to successfully complete this play? Why? Why not? ______________________________

5. What age group would find this book most appealing? Why? ______________________________

6. Do you feel that the destruction of so many characters was necessary to achieve the play's goals? Couldn't the same humor and mystery be retained without all the violence? ______________________________

7. How many of the twenty-six drawings did you predict? Which drawing was the hardest to predict/describe? ______________________________

8. Do you think the book would have been more enjoyable in color or do you feel that the black and white format accomplished the author's purpose? Please explain your thoughts. ______________________________

9. Some of my students suggested that the book be done in a 3-D or pop-out style. What do you think of this idea? Do you think that this would add or detract from the theme? ______________________________

10. The curtains behind the stage stayed the same for all the acts. Would a variety of backdrops have helped each letter's performance? What kind of backdrops would you have designed? All the letters were of the same style. Would you have changed them to Roman, Gothic or some other style? ______________________________

Vexing Vocabulary

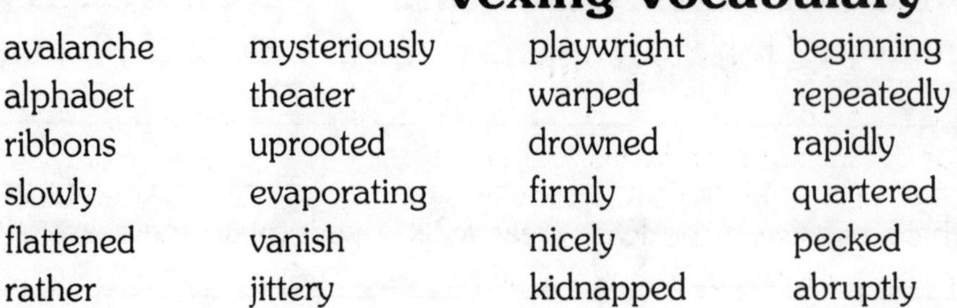

avalanche
alphabet
ribbons
slowly
flattened
rather
mysteriously
theater
uprooted
evaporating
vanish
jittery
playwright
warped
drowned
firmly
nicely
kidnapped
beginning
repeatedly
rapidly
quartered
pecked
abruptly

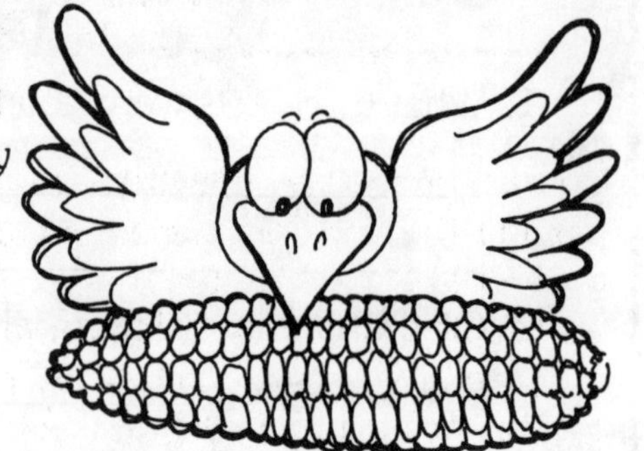

Design a sentence that contains these two words without losing its logic.
Example: pecked—vanish
I watched the corn vanish as the bird pecked at each kernel.

avalanche—jittery

____

mysteriously—uprooted

____

firmly—ribbons

____

abruptly—evaporating

____

flattened—beginning

____

nicely—theater

____

kidnapped—quartered

____

alphabet—vanish

____

pecked—rather

____

Pick five pairs of your own and complete your sentences on the back of this page.

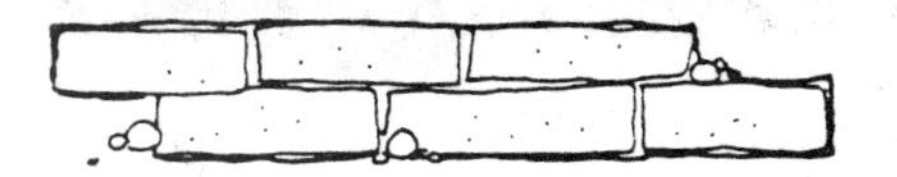

Vocabulary Buildings

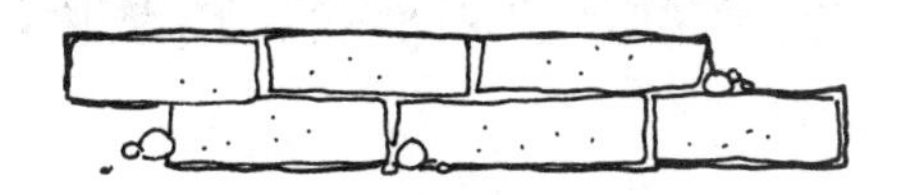

Drills for Skills

You are a spelling construction worker. Your job is to build towers that spell words. You do this by placing the spelling pieces on top of each other. We originally cut out our towers on inch-by-inch graph paper and pasted them together to make our word tower answers. Now we write our answers on the blank bars provided on the right of each set of building blocks. How many words of three or more letters can you create by putting these spelling word block pieces on top of each other? Use the following page's blank master to design spelling bars of your own. See if you can find twenty words using your bars and twenty words using the bars below.

1	2	3	4	5
R	I	F	O	S
E	N	L	R	T

6	7	8	9	10
E	I	O	P	A
S	N	N	R	R
T	G	E	E	E

11	12	13	14	15
S	P	V	A	A
O	O	E	T	B
R	R	N	E	L
T	T	T	D	B

16	17	18	19	20
D	A	E	T	N

Building Towers for 3 to 9-letter Words

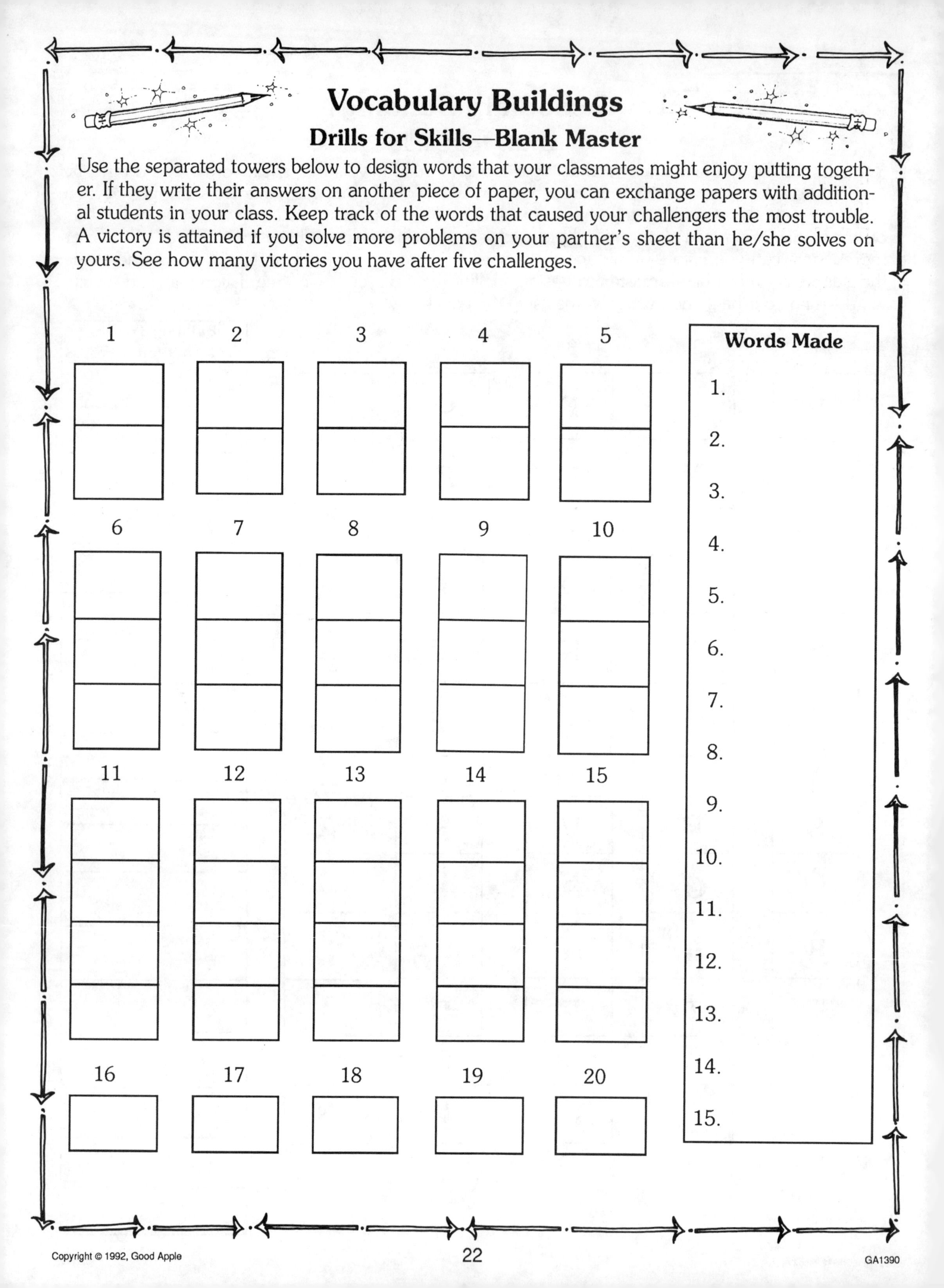

Vocabulary Buildings

Drills for Skills—Blank Master

Use the separated towers below to design words that your classmates might enjoy putting together. If they write their answers on another piece of paper, you can exchange papers with additional students in your class. Keep track of the words that caused your challengers the most trouble. A victory is attained if you solve more problems on your partner's sheet than he/she solves on yours. See how many victories you have after five challenges.

1 2 3 4 5

6 7 8 9 10

11 12 13 14 15

16 17 18 19 20

Words Made

1.
2.
3.
4.
5.
6.
7.
8.
9.
10.
11.
12.
13.
14.
15.

Character Design

Ideas and Illustrations

It is now your turn to imitate the artwork of Chris Van Allsburg's *Alphabet Theater*. There are four numbers and five letters drawn for you below. Draw what you think would happen to each number and letter in *The Z Was Zapped, Part II*. Next to each number and letter is a blank box so you can design an additional idea from scratch for each letter and number. Record the word description for each drawing next to it.

A		**C**		**D**	
T		**R**		**8**	
3		**7**		**4**	

Your Two Best Ideas

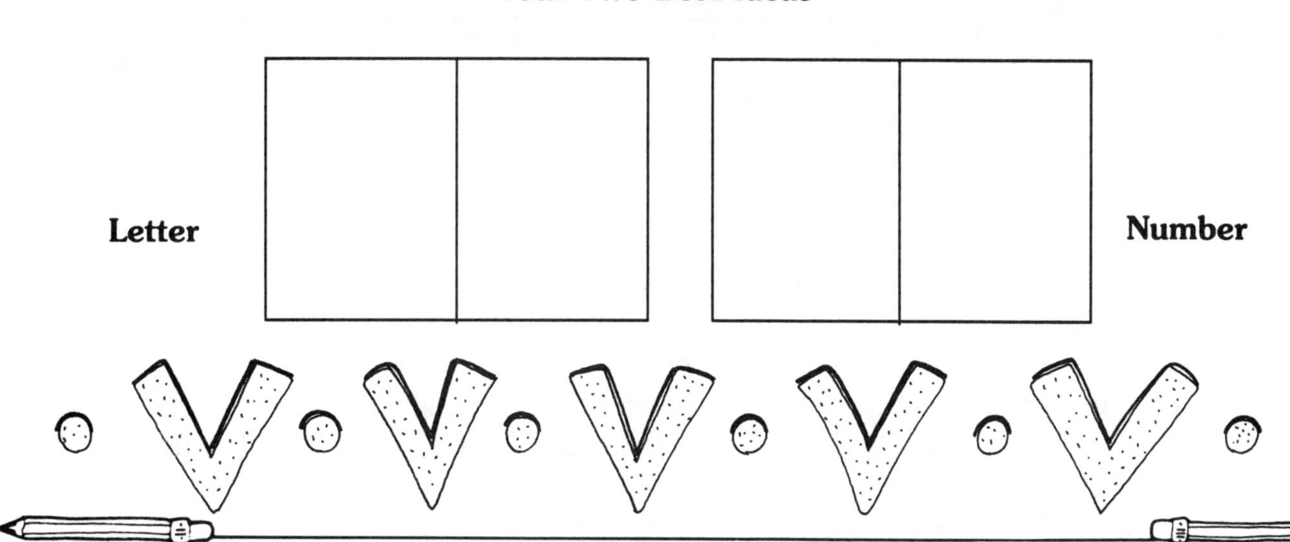

1·2·3 Brainsearching Ideas 1·2·3

Short-Term Project

Teachers are always telling children to use both sides of their brains and to search their brains for the most creative and unusual ideas. In this activity you will be looking for common answers, as well as not so common ones—three of each to be exact. Try to look at each problem with a different or unusual outlook. Examples are given for the first three brain searchers. A list of brainsearching challenges follow this activity.

Brain searcher topic: Things you can't stand

Common ideas (Please complete the example.)

1. spinach/crying babies/needles/homework
2. ______________________________
3. ______________________________

Unique ideas

1. an egg/baby-sitters/Jell-O/string
2. ______________________________
3. ______________________________

Brain searcher topic ______________________________

Common ideas

1. ______________________________
2. ______________________________
3. ______________________________

Unique ideas

1. ______________________________
2. ______________________________
3. ______________________________

Brain searcher topic ______________________________

Common ideas

1. ______________________________
2. ______________________________
3. ______________________________

Unique ideas

1. ______________________________
2. ______________________________
3. ______________________________

Here are some brainsearching ideas. Select the ones that you and your classmates will find challenging. (Check examples above.) After completing the lesson, design five brain searchers of your own—things that scream, smell, paint, fly, jump, rise, record, have springs, have holes/wholes, you can dunk, can be cut, are green, can be combined; things you can do with a toothpick, comb, shoe, cookie, bowling ball, string. Illustrate your best common and unique thoughts.

Research and Teacher Suggestions

1. I hope Chris Van Allsburg doesn't get upset with this suggestion. Write words that each character in *The Z Was Zapped* will say when he/she appears on stage.
2. Write a play for the Number Theater. This time numbers will appear on stage. Pick the numbers from one to ten and have something unique happen to each one. Try themes a little bit different from Chris Van Allsburg's theme: one feels wonderful, two wears a tutu, three strikes out. Be ready to explain your player's action in relation to the number presented.
3. Design a card inviting someone to the Alphabet Theater's newest production.
4. Create a playbill for the alphabet theater's *The Z Was Zapped.*
5. Imagine you are Siskel and Ebert. Write two reviews of *The Z Was Zapped* in a format presentation similar to theirs. Your teacher might assign each class member a partner. Use three Chris Van Allsburg books of your choice to make a mini review show. Perform your presentation in front of your classmates. Use drawings and slides to make your presentation more professional.
6. *Variety* is a theatrical newspaper. Write the front page and feature *The Z Was Zapped* as one of the key stories.
7. Research theater and presentation styles from the Greeks to Middle Ages in England to the present day theaters. Write a theater in New York, London, San Francisco or Chicago for playbills and posters. You might get lucky. Ask your local video store for some of their movie display posters. Draw your version of the poster next to the original and display them in your school hallway.
8. Public broadcasting had a show called *Backstage*. Do an imaginary interview with one of your favorite recording stars at the intermission of one of his/her concerts. Set the locale, ask questions about songs that were just sung and examine some of the things backstage that are needed for a show to be successful.
9. Very few children have seen a stage play. Research what children's theater is available in your area. Invite one of the organizers to your school to highlight this year's plays. See if he/she can bring some of the performers for a question and answer period. Cut up the announcement pamphlet and expand the advertisement for each presentation.
10. Make a clothesline of alphabet theater letter characters and numbers.
11. Stage miniaturization is a fantastic hands-on use of a person's art skills. Research this subject. Design a model of something that would be miniaturized and present it to your classmates. Maybe you can find an old sea captain who builds ships in bottles.
12. Make a list of the ten things that could go wrong with a stage play. Make five funny and five serious. Give solutions or preventive measures for each suggestion.
13. One of the easiest plays to perform is called *Sharing Letters*. Two people sit side by side and talk to each other through letters that were written back and forth.

Write Like a Master

The theme for these story starters will concern your involvement with the famous Alphabet Theater featured in this Chris Van Allsburg selection. Whether you are writing about an actor/actress, director, stagehand, technician or member of the audience, try to write as if you were that person.

Story Starter I

The curtain is halfway up and all the audience can see is the bottom half of each actor. Someone said the curtain motor burned out. The papers will make a laughing stock of me, the director, in tomorrow morning's edition. There doesn't seem to be any answer to this problem unless ____

Story Starter II

This is my first acting job. I am the letter *A* in the Alphabet Theater's newest presentation. My job is an important one. I am supposed to____

Story Starter III

My lights add magic to every play that appears in this theater. *Peter Pan* was my best work. The way I put the lights on the alligator scared everyone in the audience. My lighting actually made people think that Peter Pan was ____

Story Starter IV

I am Bruno the Great, magician of speed and time. That is, I was a great magician until the day I made a little girl from the audience disappear in my magic act. It is not funny! I was doing my normal routine. I called a child up to the stage to help with the disappearing box trick. She got in the box. I said "presto-otserp" (that's *presto* backwards). I opened the box and ____

Story Starter V

I love playing different characters. One minute I'm an older lady, the next a teenage girl. Acting lessons helped, but most of my ideas come from ____

STORY STARTERS

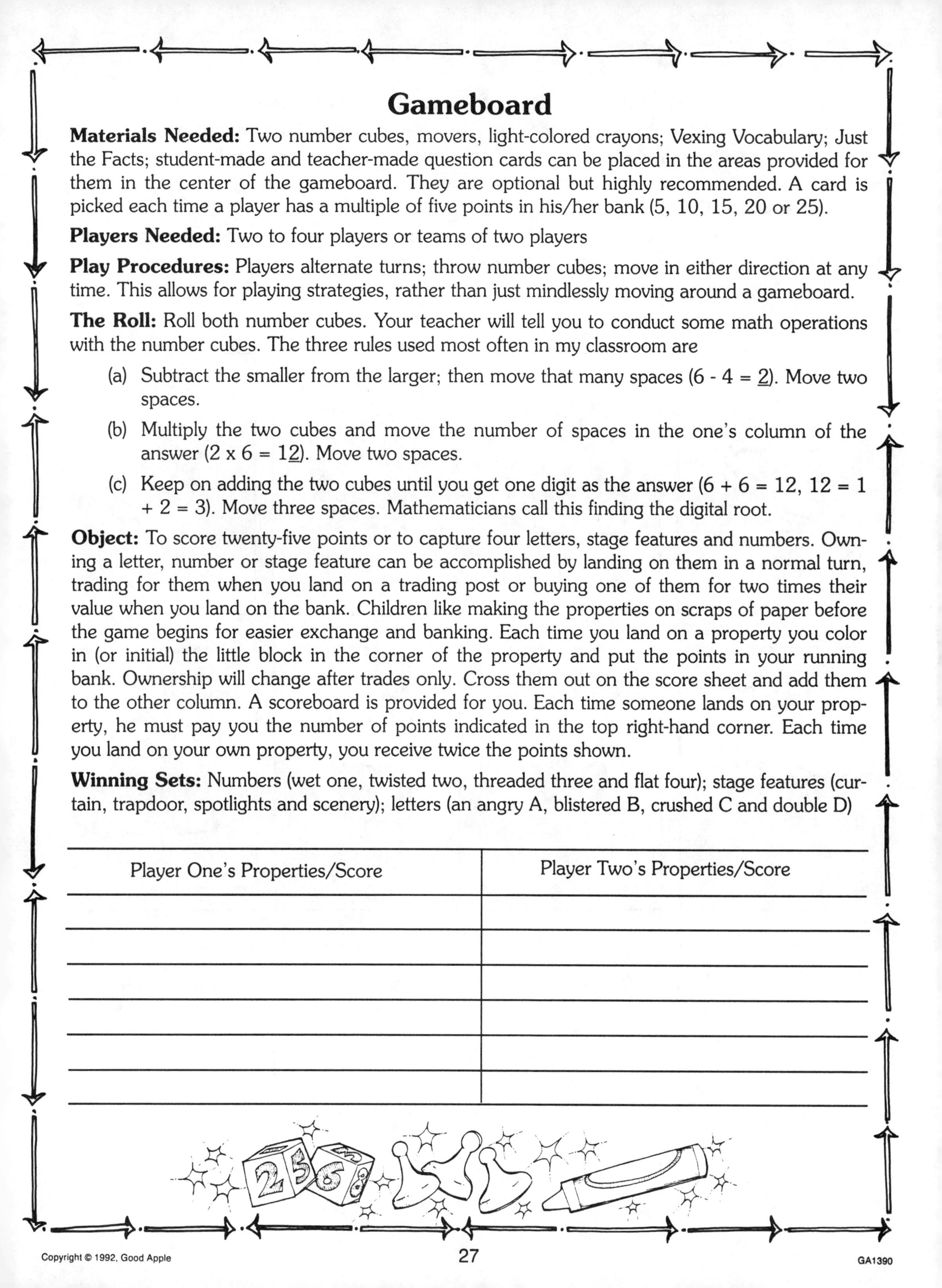

Gameboard

Materials Needed: Two number cubes, movers, light-colored crayons; Vexing Vocabulary; Just the Facts; student-made and teacher-made question cards can be placed in the areas provided for them in the center of the gameboard. They are optional but highly recommended. A card is picked each time a player has a multiple of five points in his/her bank (5, 10, 15, 20 or 25).

Players Needed: Two to four players or teams of two players

Play Procedures: Players alternate turns; throw number cubes; move in either direction at any time. This allows for playing strategies, rather than just mindlessly moving around a gameboard.

The Roll: Roll both number cubes. Your teacher will tell you to conduct some math operations with the number cubes. The three rules used most often in my classroom are

(a) Subtract the smaller from the larger; then move that many spaces (6 - 4 = 2). Move two spaces.

(b) Multiply the two cubes and move the number of spaces in the one's column of the answer (2 x 6 = 12). Move two spaces.

(c) Keep on adding the two cubes until you get one digit as the answer (6 + 6 = 12, 12 = 1 + 2 = 3). Move three spaces. Mathematicians call this finding the digital root.

Object: To score twenty-five points or to capture four letters, stage features and numbers. Owning a letter, number or stage feature can be accomplished by landing on them in a normal turn, trading for them when you land on a trading post or buying one of them for two times their value when you land on the bank. Children like making the properties on scraps of paper before the game begins for easier exchange and banking. Each time you land on a property you color in (or initial) the little block in the corner of the property and put the points in your running bank. Ownership will change after trades only. Cross them out on the score sheet and add them to the other column. A scoreboard is provided for you. Each time someone lands on your property, he must pay you the number of points indicated in the top right-hand corner. Each time you land on your own property, you receive twice the points shown.

Winning Sets: Numbers (wet one, twisted two, threaded three and flat four); stage features (curtain, trapdoor, spotlights and scenery); letters (an angry A, blistered B, crushed C and double D)

Player One's Properties/Score	Player Two's Properties/Score

Game Card Property Pieces

On this page are the twelve game pieces for *The Z Was Zapped*. Cut them out and place them on oaktag to prolong their usability. Place a little box next to the gameboard as a storage area. Each time someone lands on an appropriate board space, he receives points and one of the game cards to verify property ownership. It also makes property trading much easier. The next time you play the game, design your own game card property pieces. Design a gameboard and create your own educational board game. Pick a theme. Then try to add important facts and intellectual flavor to your game.

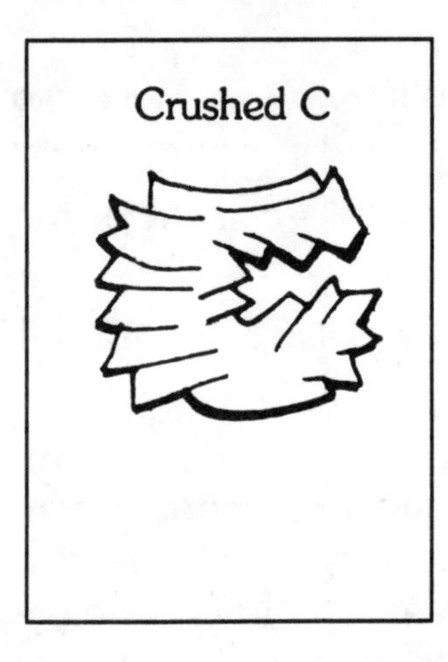

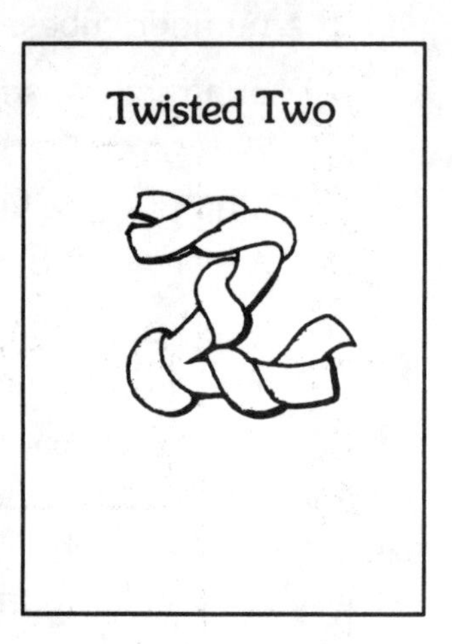

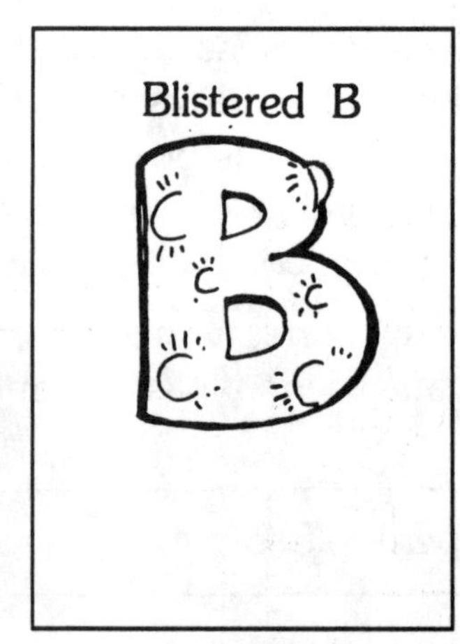

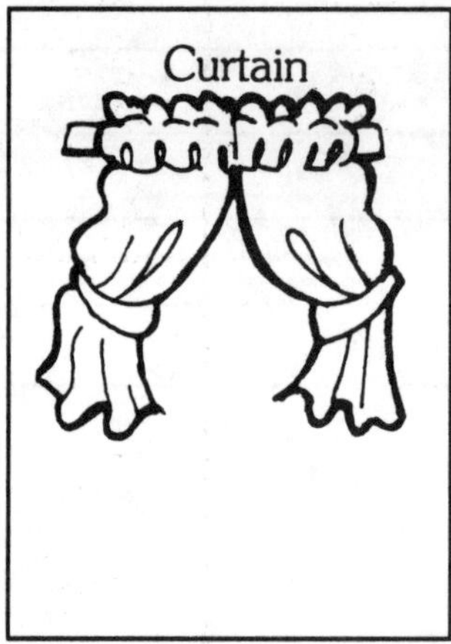

A Stage of Letters and Numbers

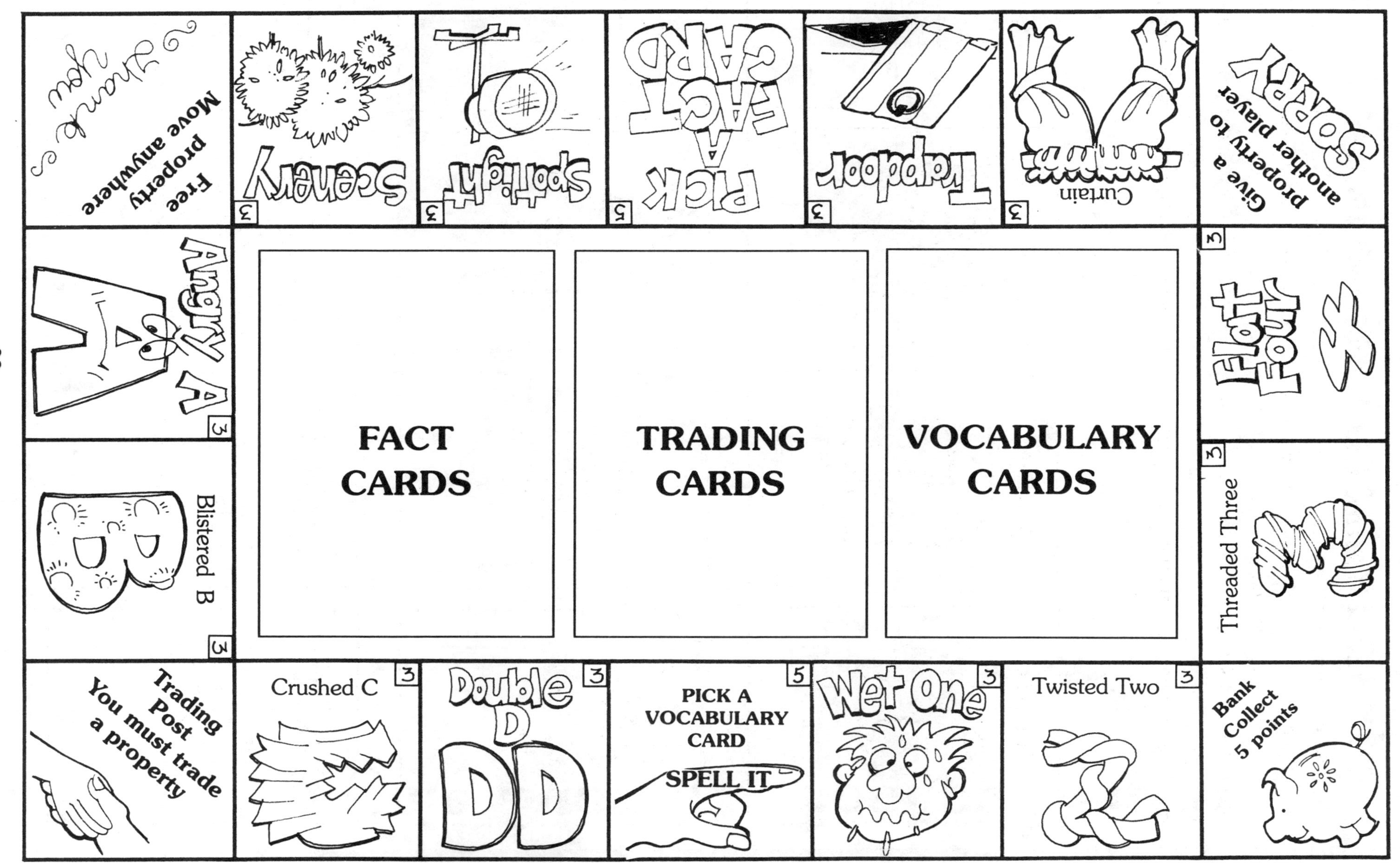

Strange Accident Silent Speech

The Stranger

Fooling Nature

First Discoveries

Welcome Guest

Changing Seasons

Quiet Manner Recovering Victim

Lead-Ins to Literature

(Read this next paragraph like you were doing a TV commercial for a book or movie.)
Do you like a good mystery? Do you like things you just can't figure out? Do you like characters that are somewhat strange but likable? Do you like odd and unexplainable situations? If you like all these things, then don't read this book. Just kidding! It all starts with a strange car accident. The victim is brought to the home of the people who hit him with their car. Things around the home start changing, but nothing near the home does. Could it be because of the stranger that is recovering there? I don't know. Why don't you read the story and make your prediction of what actually happened?

1. When I heard the title *The Stranger*, a man in a trench coat standing under a streetlight came to mind. The night was dreary and he was smoking a cigarette. He was waiting to meet someone. The person was late. Finish my thoughts and then tell/indicate what you were thinking about when you heard the title of this story.

___

___

2. Children are always told not to talk to strangers. Why is this a good rule? Why then would you bring a stranger to your house after an accident rather than letting him recuperate in a hospital? See if your mind says "Don't do it" when they decide to take the stranger back to their home.

___

___

3. Which do you think makes a better setting for a mysterious stranger story–a lonely country house, a third-floor apartment, a cabin in the woods or a single home in a quiet neighborhood? Please explain your selection. Suggest two other settings that will add mystery to the story?

___

___

4. Would you want a person with strange, unexplainable powers living in your house? What would be the benefits? What would be the drawbacks of having such a guest?

___

___

5. The stranger in this story is not a child. Would the story have even greater interest to it if it were a child that was brought home and had these mystical powers?

___

___

6. Who is the "strangest stranger" that you ever met? Why?

___

Just the Facts

1. What was the name of the family that took the stranger in after the car accident? ________
2. Why was the stranger a good worker? ________
3. Where did the car accident take place? ________
4. What did the stranger seem to lose because of the accident? ________
5. What message was left on the window? ________
6. As long as the stranger stayed at the house, what seemed to be delayed? ________
7. Who assisted the family while they were taking care of the stranger? ________
8. What changed color when the stranger blew on it? ________
9. The way the stranger looked at everything with a quizzical face seemed to suggest the stranger was ________.
10. What did the farmer notice about the land around his farm? ________
11. The stranger seemed to have the ability to talk to ________.
12. When people hit something on a country road, they usually think that it is a ________.

Write two facts about each of these topics.

Farm Work ________

Changing Seasons ________

The Accident ________

Amnesia ________

Medical Care ________

Strange Feelings ________

What Is Your Opinion?

1. Most mystery stories have shadowy, mysterious illustrations. Chris Van Allsburg's illustrations are vivid, bright and colorful. Do you think this adds to the mystery or makes it less scary? Do you think this is his purpose for designing the illustrations in such a manner? ______________

2. Do you think it was a good idea to bring the stranger home with them? ______________

3. What things in the story gave you a hint that the stranger wasn't normal? ______________

4. Who do you think the stranger really was? Explain. Do you think that this was the first time that he appeared in human form, because he really seemed out of place? ______________

5. Do you think the stranger rewarded the family with "a good season" for caring for him, or do you think that this would have happened anywhere that he lived? Please explain your thoughts. ______________

6. Many people say that they like one season over another. What is your favorite type of season/weather and would you want your season/weather to stay like that all year? Would you perfer to have all four seasons or just one or two seasons? My students laugh at me when I tell them that I'd like to have just two seasons, winter then summer. One day you are in your favorite swimming area, the next day you are sledding in a snowstorm. Can you picture the difficulties this would cause and also how much fun it could be? ______________

7. Can you think of three ways to make country roads and those roads around your school more safe? ______________

8. Can you devise three other attributes that a good stranger might have? Explain how each attribute will affect those around him/her. ______________

9. How would you have liked the story if the lead characters were twins and one changed the seasons one way, while the other ______________

Vexing Vocabulary

jammed	thump	reality	balance
fearing	lying	peeked	Katy
Bailey	parlor	thermometer	mercury
fascinated	draft	shivered	occasionally
shyly	formation	hypnotized	timid
hermit	peculiar	etched	autumn

Each sentence below contains a scrambled word that has the same meaning as a word in our vocabulary list. Unscramble the words and place the correct vocabulary words in the blanks provided below.

1. I can't believe how ... HYS... she was. ____________
2. Johnny Appleseed was at times a ... RELNO. ____________
3. I ... IESMTOMSE ... forget important facts. ____________
4. The ... EBEREZ ... chilled my whole body. ____________
5. His thumb was ... GANDEB ... in the door. ____________
6. LAFL ... is my favorite season. ____________
7. She ... OHOSK ... all night and didn't know why. ____________
8. Bees always ... DAZEMA ... me in science class. ____________
9. The ... RLOIOVMGIN ... was dusty and seemed unused. ____________
10. It is a talent to be able to ... WARD ... on glass. ____________

Write ten scrambled word sentences of your own in the blanks below. Use the remaining vocabulary words or give your partner new words that are possible answers.

1. ____
2. ____
3. ____
4. ____
5. ____
6. ____
7. ____
8. ____
9. ____
10. ____

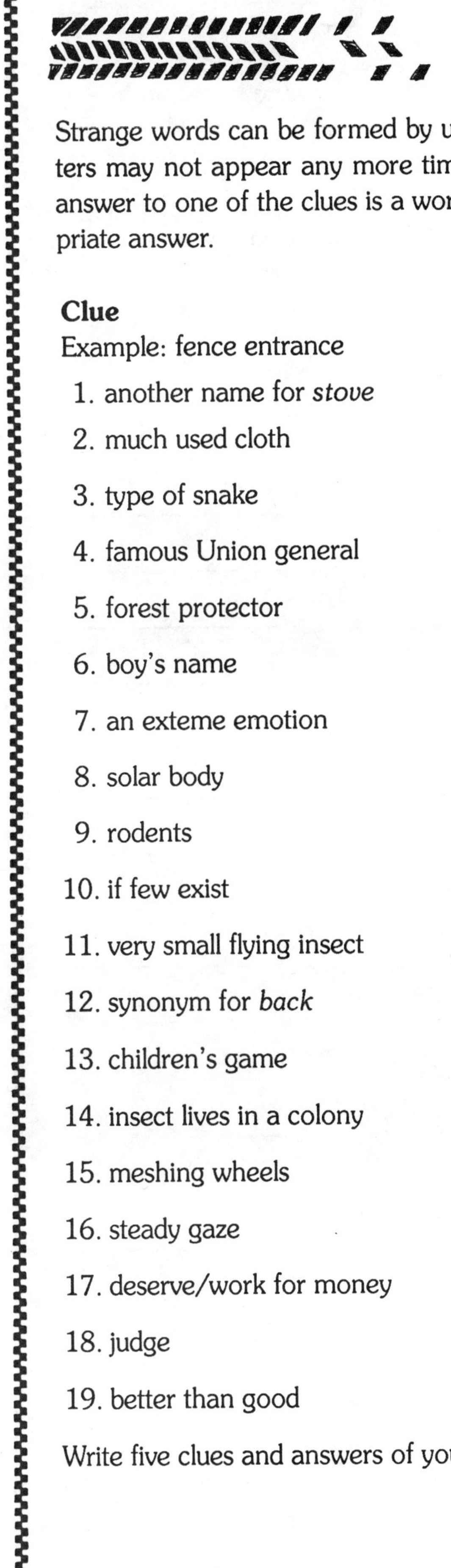

Strange Words
Drills for Skills

Strange words can be formed by using the letters in the word *stranger* to form new words. Letters may not appear any more times than in the original word. Therefore, if you think that the answer to one of the clues is a word that has three *R*'s in it, you know to look for a more appropriate answer.

Clue	**Answer Using the Letters in *Stranger***
Example: fence entrance	gate
1. another name for *stove*	______________________
2. much used cloth	______________________
3. type of snake	______________________
4. famous Union general	______________________
5. forest protector	______________________
6. boy's name	______________________
7. an exteme emotion	______________________
8. solar body	______________________
9. rodents	______________________
10. if few exist	______________________
11. very small flying insect	______________________
12. synonym for *back*	______________________
13. children's game	______________________
14. insect lives in a colony	______________________
15. meshing wheels	______________________
16. steady gaze	______________________
17. deserve/work for money	______________________
18. judge	______________________
19. better than good	______________________

Write five clues and answers of your own on the back of this sheet.

Short-Term Project

You are writing a story about a stranger who is hit by a car and taken into the home of the people who hit him. He seems to have lost his memory. Many of his actions are a little bit odd or at least not normal. What type of vocabulary would you use to describe people, places, feelings, ideas and happenings in such a story? How powerful are your word selections? Categories for your own vocabulary selections are given below. Place a word that you would use while writing the story in the first blank. In the second blank, use an actual word from the story.

Word Usage Category	Your Powerful Word	Author's Word
Example: family name	The Brennards	The Baileys
1. word describing accident	__________	__________
2. boy's name	__________	__________
3. girl's name	__________	__________
4. doctor's name	__________	__________
5. adjective describing home	__________	__________
6. noun found on farm	__________	__________
7. adjective describing illness	__________	__________
8. powerful adverb	__________	__________
9. location	__________	__________
10. feelings of the stranger	__________	__________
11. feelings of the family	__________	__________
12. land's beauty	__________	__________
13. the harvest/work	__________	__________
14. describing uncertainty	__________	__________
15. dinner	__________	__________
16. autumn/changing season	__________	__________
17. plot/setting	__________	__________
18. author/illustrations	__________	__________

Record the story's five most powerful words on the back of this sheet.

Ideas and Illustrations

Many states pay thousands of dollars to advertising agencies to design campaigns to get tourists to visit their states. An example is "Virginia Is for Lovers." You will be asked to design ten slogans for the following states and countries. Try to focus some of your ideas on the things that happened in *The Stranger.* One of the best ideas received from my students was "Come to Pennsylvania and See Our Fields of Dreams." Make a mini illustration to go with each state's (country's) new slogan.

California	**New York**
Florida	**Ohio**
Utah	**Washington**
France	**England**

Research Suggestions

1. What are the three principal crops of your region? What are your state's leading crops? Make a mini map of your state showing the crops and industries in each section of your state. Most encyclopedias have this format for you.
2. Make a poster titled "Which One Is the Real Stranger?" Draw pictures of three strangers. Try to make each one's appearance different. Have your classmates vote on the one that they like best.
3. Design a mini mural highlighting strange and fascinating creatures of fact or fiction. Have each classmate draw three of his/her favorites on art paper. Then select the best creature from each student to be placed on the mural. Overhead projectors can be used to enlarge each person's drawing to a larger scale.
4. Many community watch programs deal with how to spot troublesome strangers. Find out what techniques are in their townspeople training program.
5. Research two-way and shortwave radios.
6. How have communciation satellites changed the way we receive information from television stations to the news to secret spy "stuff"? Write to the Federal Communications Commission in Washington, D.C., for information about starting a radio or television station. Ask them for a list of communication satellites, launch dates and what each satellite's function is.
7. Invite a member of a 4-H club to speak to your class.
8. Find out what computer data bases are available to people interested in manufacturing, agriculture/farming or mining. Have each member of your class pick a governmental department. Then write to the department with five specific questions for that department. Some examples might be:

   Defense–Can you send us a graph of this year's defense spendings?

   Interior–What areas does the Department of the Interior oversee and regulate? (This should be a standard question asked of all departments.)

   Education–Has our state funding been increased or decreased and in what areas?

   Health/Welfare–What national programs for the homeless do you coordinate? Are there chapters in my area?
9. Pick three painters, for example, Da Vinci, Raphael, Michelangelo. Make a copy of one of each's paintings. Place a Chris Van Allsburg drawing next to each one and compare their styles in a short narrative.

Teacher Suggestions

1. *Time Liner: History in Perspective* is an excellent computer program. It helps students develop professional looking, historical and personal time lines. It is produced by Tom Snyder Productions, 90 Sherman Street, Cambridge, MA 02140. Send for their educational catalog or call them at 617-876-4433. Teach your class how to design a personal, historic or story time line. Have them make one about themselves, an historic figure and singer. After they are comfortable with time lines, have them make one for two of Chris Van Allsburg's books. One book could be *The Stranger.*
2. Sunburst Communications, 29 Washington Avenue, Pleasantville, NY 10570-9971, has an outstanding collection of data bases from their Bankstreet Filer program. Ideas range from astronomy to satellites in space. We use it extensively in our school. Even if you don't have a computer in your classroom, children should be taught how to design and use a data base, as well as where to find it for their research.
3. Discuss with your class the various time zones in the United States and throughout the world. Make a time zone chart showing what five different children are doing at five locations at 1 p.m. your time.
4. Discuss with your class what jet lag is and how it affects our bodies' rhythms.
5. There is a lot of research on how light affects our mood and productivity. Take a light survey with your class and find out what types of lights are used in students' schools, homes and places of play.
6. Discuss with your class methods of identifying strangers in the neighborhood. A local police unit would gladly assist you with this presentation.
7. The injury to the stranger brings to mind the importance of CPR instruction, even to young children. Please! Please! Have your class take a mini lifesaving CPR course. So many lives could be saved, if we all knew what to do while waiting for help.
8. Many children live in areas that don't have four distinct seasons. Design mini stories titled "Not One More Day of Summer, Spring, Winter or Fall." (Pick one.) Have the children illustrate the reasons for choosing the topics they did.
9. Answer these questions about the stranger with your class. Where did the stranger come from? Why did everything seem strange to him? How could he work for hours without getting tired? What did he mean by "I'll be back"? Did he mean summer would be back or he would be back?
10. Design "I Need a Friend" T-shirts with your class.
11. Collect farm pictures for a class farm portfolio.

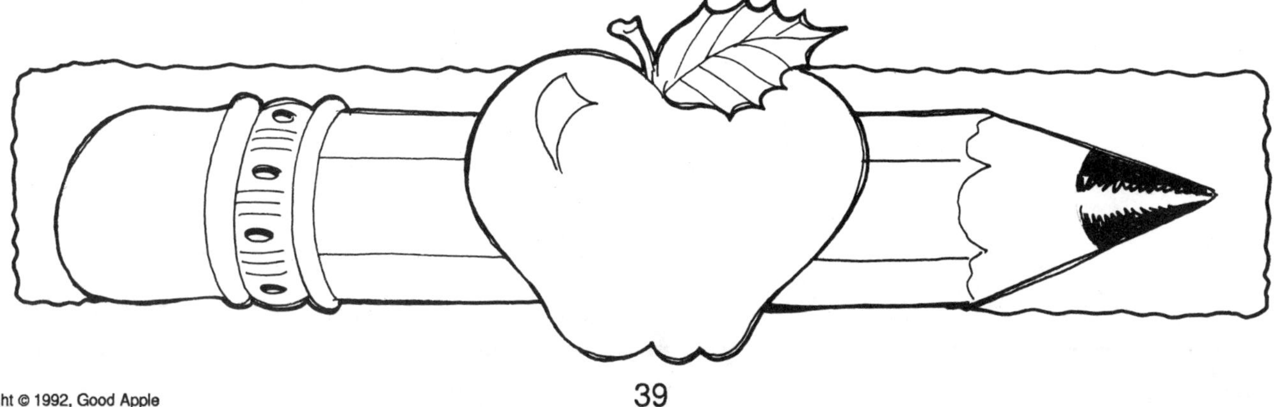

Write Like a Master

The theme for these story starters revolves around a visitor to your house, school or job. The visitor could be a family member, a friend or someone of unknown and mysterious origin.

Story Starter I

This journey is all because a strange man came to our house with what he said was a map of the long lost temple of the Egyptian Pharaoh Cheops. He said Uncle Frank left it to us in his will. I didn't even know I had an Uncle Frank. The map was found in the recently excavated tomb of Ramses II. The markings seem to indicate the location of some sort of fluid, maybe the secret embalming fluid or fluid of life of the early Egyptians. We should have questioned our strange visitor instead of just starting out on this journey. Help me move this giant slab of rock from the entrance. ____________________

____

____

____

____

Story Starter II

We always enjoyed visits to Grandma's house. Something about the smell of freshly baked bread just seemed to make her house special. We all know how much she misses Granddad and that is why we visit more often. We miss him a lot. It is hard to explain. ____________________

____

____

____

____

Story Starter III

Mom always said, "Don't talk to strangers." I don't know who I talked to, what I thought was just a lonely man sitting on a park bench. Evil magicians come in all different forms, and I found out the hard way that ____________________

____

____

____

____

Story Starter IV

Who was the most unforgettable character that you have ever met? How old was this person? What made this person interesting or different from other people that you have met? Did this person change your life or ideas in some way? ____________________

____

____

____

____

write like a master

Gameboard

Materials Needed: Two number cubes, movers, light-colored crayons; Vexing Vocabulary; Just the Facts; student-made and teacher-made question cards can be placed in the areas provided for them in the center of the gameboard. They are optional but highly recommended. A card is picked each time a player has a multiple of five points in his/her bank (5, 10, 15, 20 or 25).

Players Needed: Two to four players or teams of two players

Play Procedures: Players alternate turns; throw number cubes; move in either direction at any time. This allows for playing strategies, rather than just mindlessly moving around a gameboard.

The Roll: Roll both number cubes. Your teacher will tell you to conduct some math operation with the number cubes. The three rules used most often in my classroom are

(a) Subtract the smaller from the larger; then move that many spaces (6 - 4 = 2). Move two spaces.

(b) Multiply the two cubes and move the number of spaces in the one's column of the answer (2 x 6 = 12). Move two spaces.

(c) Keep on adding the two cubes until you get one digit as the answer (6 + 6 = 12, 12 = 1 + 2 = 3). Move three spaces. Mathematicians call this finding the digital root.

Object: To score twenty-five points or to capture four farm structures, seasons or accidents. Owning farm structures, accidents and seasons can be accomplished by landing on them in a normal turn, trading for them when you land on a trading post or buying one of them for two times their value when you land on the bank. Children like making the properties on scraps of paper before the game begins for easier exchange and banking. Each time you land on a property you color in (or initial) the little block in the corner of the property and put the points in your running bank. Ownership will change after trades only. Cross them out on the score sheet and add them to the other column. A scoreboard is provided for you. Each time someone lands on your property, he must pay you the number of points indicated in the top right-hand corner. Each time you land on your own property, you receive twice the points shown.

Winning Sets: Seasons (summer, winter, fall and spring); accidents (paper cut, broken glasses, sprain and lost tooth); farm structures (barn, silo, corral and hen coop)

Player One's Properties/Score	Player Two's Properties/Score

Game Card Property Pieces

On this page are the twelve game pieces for *The Stranger*. Cut them out and place them on oaktag to prolong their usability. Place a little box next to the gameboard as a storage area. Each time someone lands on an appropriate board space, he receives points and one of the game cards to verify property ownership. It also makes property trading much easier. The next time you play the game, design your own game card property pieces. Design a gameboard and create your own educational board game. Pick a theme. Then try to add important facts and intellectual flavor to your game.

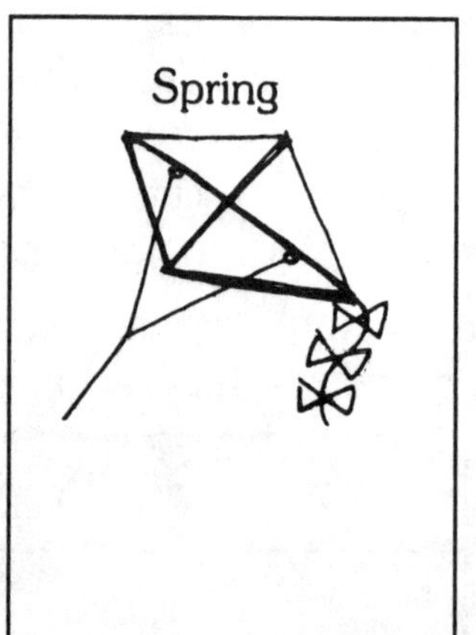

A Farm for All Seasons

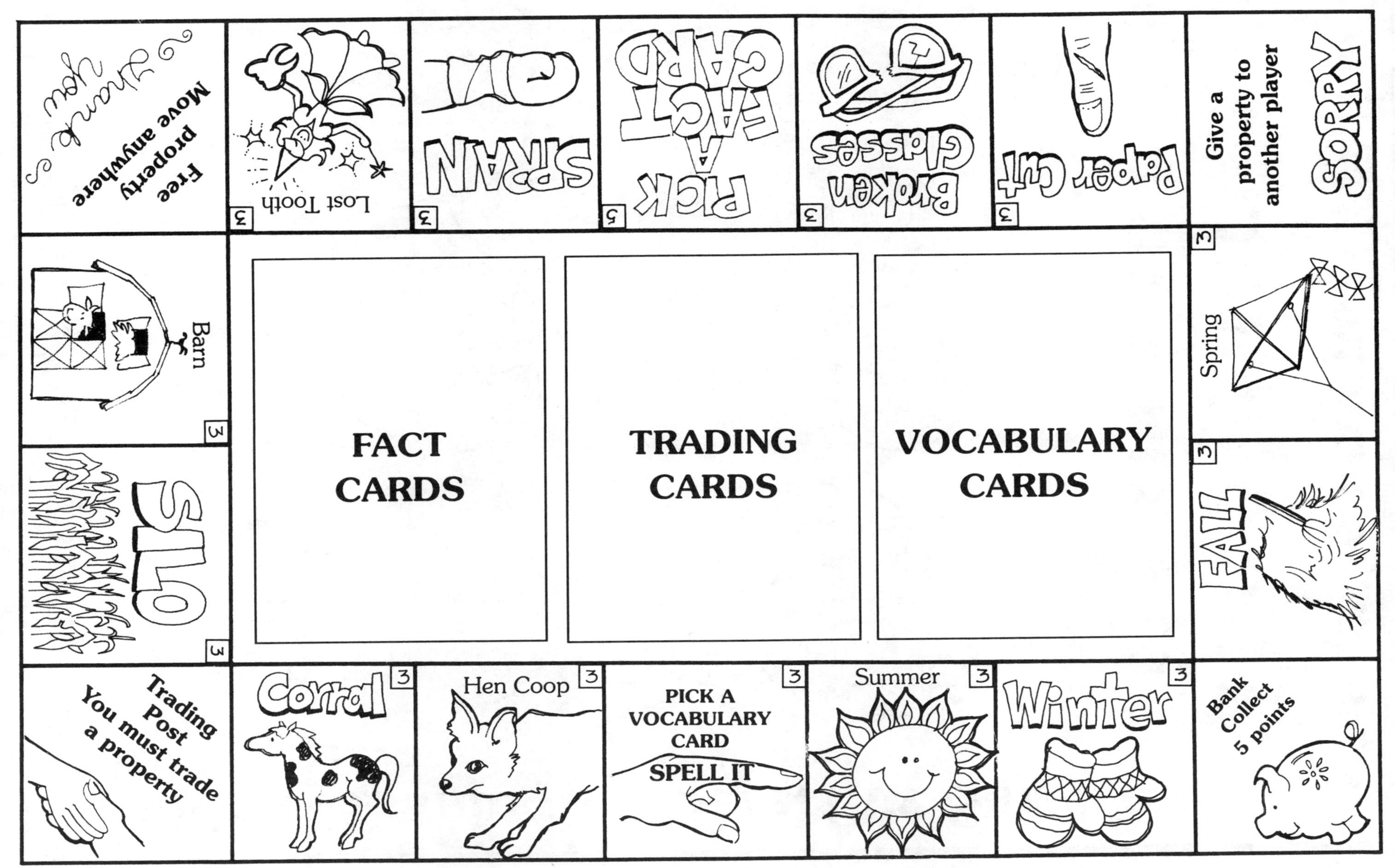

Artist's Depictions Creative Ideas

The Mysteries of Harris Burdick

Detective Services

Unsolved Mysteries

Hidden Meaning

Flights of Fancy

Imagination Starters

Lead-Ins to Literature

If you are a mystery story fanatic, you will love this book. Each page is a mystery with the smallest number of clues. Your mind has to finish each investigation that has already been started. What kind of imagination do you have? How many of the fourteen cases can you solve? Is there more than one solution to each case? Who is this guy, Harris Burdick, anyway? Maybe his cases are all a big hoax started by Chris Van Allsburg.

1. When you heard this was a book of mysteries, did you think they were the Nancy Drew, Agatha Christie, Sherlock Holmes variety of cases? Explain your thoughts, please. ________

2. Harris Burdick delivered these fourteen mysteries to Chris Van Allsburg's publisher's office. He never returned to give any additional clues or answers to the case. Can you think of three things that might have prevented him from returning for his money and almost certain fame?

3. Why do you think that Chris Van Allsburg is on this quest to solve all these mysteries? ______

4. Don't you think that Chris Van Allsburg should have gone to the police, Scotland Yard or Interpol for help rather than to children all over the world? Why do you think he thought children would be able to supply more clues to these mysteries than trained professionals?

5. Is it possible to stimulate every imagination that reads this book, as the author seems to claim in the introduction? Don't you feel that some imaginations can't be stimulated and it doesn't matter how hard authors, illustrators and teachers try? ________

6. What is the most stimulating mystery that you have heard up to this point? ________

7. How many of the fourteen mysteries do you expect to solve? On a scale of 1-10 (poor-excellent), what do you think your stick-to-itiveness rating would be? Explain. ________

8. When you see a movie or read a book, do you usually figure out things before they happen? Why do you think you can or can't do this? ________

9. What do you think is the world's greatest mystery? ________

! CLUES !

Just the Facts

1. Where did Chris Van Allsburg discover the fourteen mysteries of Harris Burdick? ________

____

2. How many years ago did Peter Wenders meet Harris Burdick? ________

3. What was in the dust-covered box that Peter Wenders showed Chris Van Allsburg? ________

____

4. What kind of voice was used in the Archie Smith story? ________

5. How many strange visitors did Archie have? ________

6. What did the third skipping stone act like? ________

7. What was the time period for the appearance of things that moved under the rug? ________

8. What did the things under the rug disturb? ________

9. What hid the railroad tracks? ________

10. How many stacks did the ocean liner have? ________

11. What was the sign that uninvited guests were arriving? ________

12. What ended up in a cathedral? ________

13. What was attacking the sleeping girl? ________

14. Where was the harp found? ________

15. Where can you find a mailbox in the story? ________

16. What was the secret number of lantern swings? ________

17. What creatures were good spellers? ________

18. What season of the year did *Just Deserts* take place? ________

19. Who were Oscar and Alphonse? ________

20. What came alive on the wall of the third-floor bedroom? ________

21. What city had some of its buildings destroyed? ________

What Is Your Opinion?

1. Can you give two reasons for the pumpkin's glow? ______________________________
2. The ship was in reverse and was still being pulled forward. What ideas would you have tried to stop it from going into the canal any further? ______________________________
3. Would you have smashed something under your living room rug before finding out what it was? ______________________________
4. What three things would you do with a come-back stone? ______________________________
5. Why do you think Peter Wenders waited so long before sharing his Harris Burdick story with Chris Van Allsburg? ______________________________
6. In most creature stories, do you think the author wants it to appear like there is more danger while you are sleeping or awake? Explain the power of both ideas in the reader's mind? ______________________________
7. Why do you think that a harp is so often picked as an instrument of mystery in so many stories? ______________________________
8. Would a different creature communicating in writing to the young girl have added any additional suspense to the caterpillar mystery? Do you think they were used because in your hand they seem soft, furry and cuddly? ______________________________
9. The house seemed to be lifting up like a rocket ship. Yet, the story was written before rocket ships were invented. Do you think that Harris Burdick could tell the future and maybe that is why he disappeared? ______________________________
10. Don't you think that the ship in *Captain Tory* would have been more scary if it were a pirate ship or Russian submarine, rather than just a schooner? ______________________________
11. The fifth chair has a nun sitting in it. Do you think the other six chairs have some sort of religious significance, or was this the only religious setting? ______________________________
12. In what story would you have liked to have been a participant? ______________________________
13. Chris Van Allsburg tells some great stories with his pictures. Why do you think we are attracted to things that have little writing but tell giant stories through their illustrations? ______________________________
14. What author, would you say, compares to Chris Van Allsburg? Please explain why you feel the way you do. ______________________________
15. Where would you have a mystery ship appear in your neighborhood? ______________________________ Why? ______________________________

Vexing Vocabulary

inspired	reproduced	publisher	fascinated
caption	voice	downright	further
cardboard	wonder	reverse	strange
lantern	schooner	appeared	engine
caterpillar	wiggle	desert	canal
fifth	warned	thought	Venice

Each clue below will generate a word that rhymes with one of the words from the story. Place the answer to the clue in column one. Then put the vocabulary word it rhymes with in column two.

Clue	Answer	Vocabulary Word
Example: Put in order	arrange	strange
1. Dennis the ______	______	______
2. real friend	______	______
3. purchased	______	______
4. opposite of *length*	______	______
5. half laugh	______	______
6. cloud noise	______	______
7. judged 1-10	______	______
8. not loose	______	______
9. after dinner treat	______	______
10. practicing doctor	______	______

Write five clues from your school reading vocabulary list. Place them in the spaces below. Challenge a classmate to find your clue and the rhyming vocabulary word.

1. ______ ______ ______
2. ______ ______ ______
3. ______ ______ ______
4. ______ ______ ______
5. ______ ______ ______

Can you write two clues for vocabulary words above that we might have overlooked? Try this with another vocabulary list that appears in this book–fish, bird or tree names.

Drills for Skills I

You have probably studied acrostic poetry with your classroom teacher. This involves placing the letters in a word downward and trying to think up a line of poetry that will describe the total word that you have written downward. Try this with the word *mystery*. Writing one descriptive line starting with each letter. See if you can do this in rhyme form.

M ______________________________

Y ______________________________

S ______________________________

T ______________________________

E ______________________________

R ______________________________

Y ______________________________

A double acrostic is even more challenging. A letter appears in the beginning of each line and at the end of the same line. You are challenged to describe the downward word. This time a beginning and ending letter for each sentence is given for you.

S ______________________________ S

T ______________________________ T

R ______________________________ R

A ______________________________ A

N ______________________________ N

G ______________________________ G

E ______________________________ E

An easier way to work with the double acrostic technique is to just find words that begin and end with the letters in the downward word. The words do not have to relate to the downward word. Try these three; then write your own.

S	______	S	L	______	L	P	______	P
C	______	C	E	______	E	L	______	L
H	______	H	T	______	T	E	______	E
O	______	O	T	______	T	A	______	A
O	______	O	E	______	E	S	______	S
L	______	L	R	______	R	E	______	E

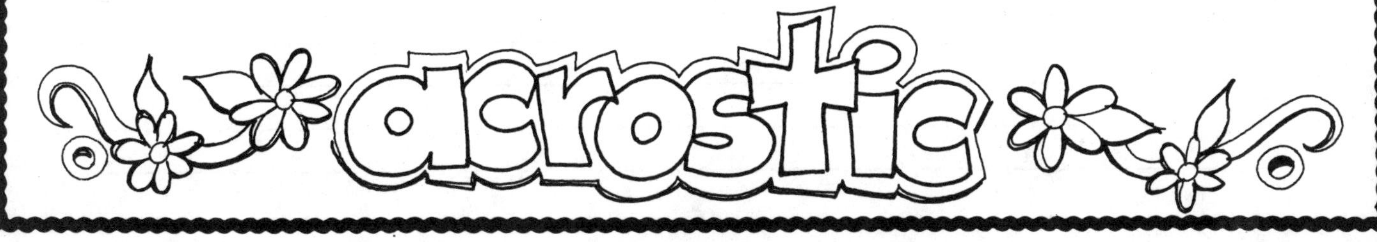

What's in a Name?

Drills for Skills II

The What's in a Name? game can be used during a car trip, at a party or in a classroom. Clues are given for words that can be made by using the letters in your name. No letter can be used more times than it appears in your name. If a letter does not appear in your name, you may not use it as part of your secret word. Each clue will help you to find a word that is made up of some of the letters in *Harris Burdick*. Five spaces have been provided for your Harris Burdick clues.

Clues

1. a type of building material ... found in Harris Burdick?
2. a great white ... found in Harris Burdick?
3. snow glider ... found in Harris Burdick?
4. a bug spray ... found in Harris Burdick?
5. a dry area term or deodorant ... found in Harris Burdick?
6. a plover ... found in Harris Burdick?
7. a part of the eye or flower ... found in Harris Burdick?
8. a shoe cleaner or hair fixer ... found in Harris Burdick?
9. a piece of furniture ... found in Harris Burdick?
10. not soft ... found in Harris Burdick?
11. baby goat or child ... found in Harris Burdick?
12. a red-skinned plant root ... found in Harris Burdick?
13. foaming at the mouth dog ... found in Harris Burdick?
14. ______________________ found in Harris Burdick?
15. ______________________ found in Harris Burdick?
16. ______________________ found in Harris Burdick?
17. ______________________ found in Harris Burdick?
18. ______________________ found in Harris Burdick?

Answers

1. brick
2. ______________________
3. ______________________
4. ______________________
5. ______________________
6. ______________________
7. ______________________
8. ______________________
9. ______________________
10. ______________________
11. ______________________
12. ______________________
13. ______________________
14. ______________________
15. ______________________
16. ______________________
17. ______________________
18. ______________________

Write a famous person's name in this blank: ______________________. Generate three easy clues and three hard clues using the letters in the famous name that you selected.

1. ______________________
2. ______________________
3. ______________________
4. ______________________
5. ______________________
6. ______________________

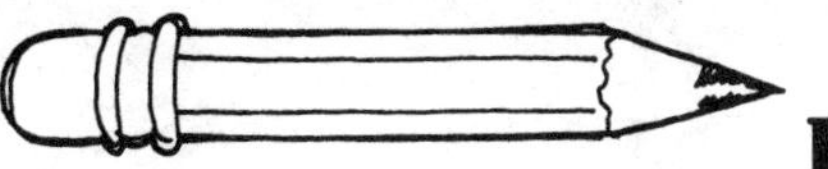

Ideas and Illustrations

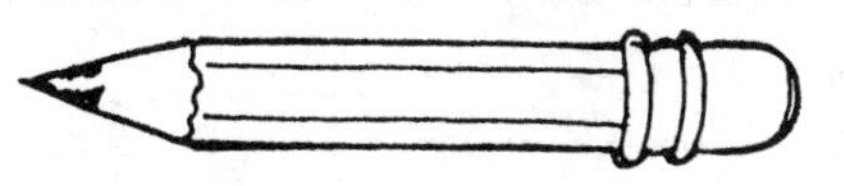

What kind of story starter expert are you? Do you feel more comfortable expressing your ideas through your drawings or your creative writing? Imagine that you are Harris Burdick and have a portfolio of your best story starters. Eight themes are given to you below. Think of a story starting thought for each theme and draw its accompanying picture next to it.

Brief Story Lead-In	**Drawing**
A Dog Mystery Lead-in: ____________________ ____________________ ____________________	
A Car with Fog Around It Lead-in: ____________________ ____________________ ____________________	
A Ladder into the Clouds Lead-in: ____________________ ____________________ ____________________	
A Pond with a Talking Fish Lead-in: ____________________ ____________________ ____________________	
An Apple Suspended in Air Lead-in: ____________________ ____________________ ____________________	
Man Hitting Baseball Without a Bat Lead-in: ____________________ ____________________ ____________________	
A Strange Hat Lead-in: ____________________ ____________________ ____________________	
Horse Sense Lead-in: ____________________ ____________________ ____________________	

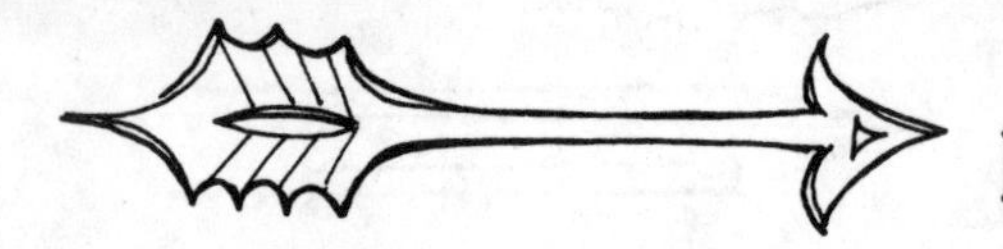

Poetic Story Starters

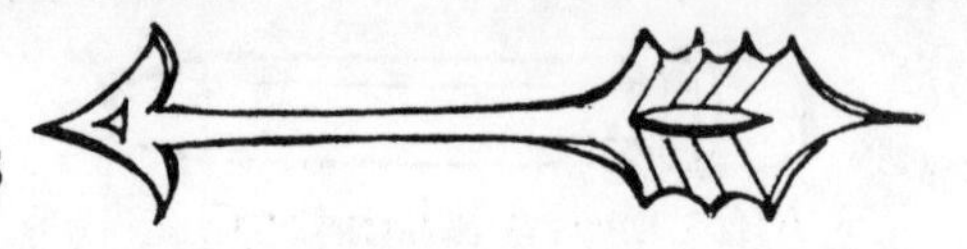

Short-Term Project

I wonder if it would be possible to introduce each story starter with a couplet, tercet or quatrain and not lose the author's intended mystery of picture and words? The fourteen story starter titles are below and on the following page. Review each picture before creating a verse that will cause readers to investigate the mystery of each picture. Some are completed for you as examples. See if you can create additional verses for those already given to you. Try drawing your own story starters and writing verses to pique your readers' imaginations.

Archie Smith, Boy Wonder

They flew in the sleeping boy's window, two by two. It was my guess that they had some mischief to do.

Under the Rug

____

____

____

____

A Strange Day in July

____

____

____

____

Missing in Venice

____

____

____

____

Another Place, Another Time

____

____

____

____

Uninvited Guests

____

____

____

____

The Harp

____

____

____

____

Mr. Linden's Library
Children should know
There are places in the library
Where no one should go.

The Seven Chairs
What was her mission?
Who sent her there?
Why did she travel
On a chair in the air?

The Third-Floor Bedroom

Just Desert

Captain Tory
Three waves of the lantern in the dark of the night
Brought an eerie schooner into the light.

Oscar and Alphonse

The House on Maple Street

Place your imaginative picture on 11" x 14" (27.94 x 35.56 cm) paper; then place your descriptive verse on the lines below.

Research Suggestions

1. Chris Van Allsburg seems to have quite a few references to water and the ocean in his story starters. Find out why living in Providence, Rhode Island, would influence him to use the sea in a majority of his themes. His book *The Wreck of the Zephyr* also appears to show his nautical roots.
2. What kind of formal art training did Chris Van Allsburg have? Who were some of his teachers? Is there a *Who's Who in Art/Illustrators* that would contain this information?
3. Copy one of the pictures that you enjoyed. Draw a scene that would have happened just before the picture you selected. Follow the book drawing with a drawing of what would have happened immediately after the picture you selected.
4. Put together a booklet called "The Mysteries of __________" (your name). Even if you aren't a great artist, you can use cutouts to enhance your ideas. Write some short spur-the-imagination sentences for each picture, design a cover and get ready for the same critical success that Chris Van Allsburg has received for his ideas. Work with a partner and call your booklet "The Mysteries of __________ and __________."
5. What famous artists also used black and white as their medium of choice? Compare their drawings to the drawings of Chris Van Allsburg in *Jumanji* and *The Mysteries of Harris Burdick*. Write a short critique comparing two of the artists. Use two drawings to make your points understood.
6. Set up a display table of books that were written and illustrated by the same person. Were you able to find just as many men and women who are authors/illustrators? Take a survey of the people who read each book. A great number of questions can be discussed. Was the author a better storyteller or illustrator? Were the story and pictures of equal quality? Etc.
7. Check with your local agencies for how a missing person's report should be made out. What laws pertain to the search for a missing person? Make out a missing person's report for someone in your family. Having a loved one missing is no joking matter. It is the author's hope that understanding what quick actions can be taken if a person is missing, might be the key to a speedy recovery. Knowing how to present accurate information can and will save loved ones from injury and worse.
8. Research the history of ships. Make a pictograph (time line) showing various dates/eras and a drawing or cutout above the date of a ship that sailed at that time period.
9. Make a mural of "The World's Best Mystery Writers." List two of their best books and illustrate a scene from each story.
10. The Baby Sitter's Club is a much-read series of books. Make a poster advertising "The Mystery Writers' Club." Focus on club membership rules, exciting new stories and famous adventures of the past. Then do this for the baby-sitter's adventures.

Teacher Suggestions

1. Diorama's are often overused, but I enjoyed my students' projects surrounding their favorite mystery stories.
2. "The Great Detective Presentation" involves having your students present themselves as "the world's greatest detective." Each student must present a case that he has solved and present three props that were an important part of his case's solution.
3. Investigate "The Great Cities by the Water." Compare the advantages and disadvantages of living near an ocean, river or lake. Have each person in the class present his choice for the world's most outstanding ocean, river and lake city. An 11" x 14" (27.94 x 35.56 cm) drawing/creative cutouts of the great cities should accompany the presentation. Tally the results of your class' choices. Write the three cities that were chosen and plan an imaginary trip or day to spend in each one.
4. Every community has a group of artists who would be willing to share their talents with a group of students. Write to four of them and ask for simple lessons like: A. How to draw facial features, B. Giving dimension to your drawings, C. Still life, D. Movement in art, E. Famous landscape or seascape styles, F. Art history, G. Cartography, H. Advertising techniques in art.
5. Discuss with your class the author's/illustrator's ability to hook you on his presentation with a limited number of words and drawings. Have your class find good and poor examples of this technique and justify his point of view. Have your students comment on how this author or illustrator might improve on his written or drawn presentation.
6. A great many artist and creativity debates can be derived from the Harris Burdick drawings. Discuss, contrast and compare points of view on the following topics:
   a. Sea Lovers vs. Land Lovers
   b. Black and White Drawings vs. Colored Drawings
   c. Elaborative vs. Simplicity in Art and Fashion
   d. Fantasy vs. Science Fiction
   e. How Dreams Might Interfere with Reality
   f. The Importance of Fairy Tales
7. Not one single monster was used by Chris Van Allsburg in his drawings. He, nonetheless, created a sometimes frightening look at those things around us. Discuss with the class the pros and cons of throwing monsters out of all children's literature. Is it necessary to scare young children with ghastly stories of supposed fact and fiction?
8. Research with your class the publications that accept children's art efforts.
9. Conduct a *What's My Line* show with students from your class claiming to be the real Harris Burdick. Have students ask this panel of would-be Harris Burdicks questions about their artwork, ideas and story starter mysteries. This works well with characters from history, also. They have to have good facts about their character ... a vote conclusion?

Write Like a Master

The theme for these story starters is the strange appearance of a man or woman with creative ideas. He/She wants you to look at and evaluate his/her work. You are not too sure how to deal with this stranger.

Story Starters I

How did you change into my mother and then my best friend? You used your soon-to-be-patented person-a-gram! That's amazing! You can actually change into the person someone is thinking about or give a message, flowers, card or greeting to a person as the actual person sending the item? Can anyone who uses your device do the same thing? How does this revolutionary device work? ____

____

____

____

Story Starter II

I don't want to secretly look into your briefcase. This is the United States Patent Office. If you have something to show me, please, put it on the desk. We must take a picture of it for our records. (Man opens box ... blinding light fills room.) Please ask it to ______________________

____

____

____

____

Story Starter III

Put this hat on and point at any object in the room. See how it makes the object move in the opposite direction. It takes a while to master, but I can now move objects up to ten pounds in weight. I am now trying to move people. If I succeed, no one could tackle me in a football game. It works on a simple principle. The hat hides______________________________

____

____

____

Story Starter IV

This is my most powerful solution ever. It molds into a plastic putty. You put this putty in the bottom of your shoe. Anchor your toes in it and think of ______________________

____

____

____

____

write like a master

Gameboard

Materials Needed: Two number cubes, movers, light-colored crayons; Vexing Vocabulary; Just the Facts; student-made and teacher-made question cards can be placed in the areas provided for them in the center of the gameboard. They are optional but highly recommended. A card is picked each time a player has a multiple of five points in his/her bank (5, 10, 15, 20 or 25).

Players Needed: Two to four players or teams of two players

Play Procedures: Players alternate turns; throw number cubes; move in either direction at any time. This allows for playing strategies, rather than just mindlessly moving around a gameboard.

The Roll: Roll both number cubes. Your teacher will tell you to conduct some math operations with the number cubes. The three rules used most often in my classroom are

(a) Subtract the smaller from the larger; then move that many spaces (6 - 4 = 2). Move two spaces.

(b) Multiply the two cubes and move the number of spaces in the one's column of the answer (2 x 6 = 12). Move two spaces.

(c) Keep on adding the two cubes until you get one digit as the answer (6 + 6 = 12, 12 = 1 + 2 = 3). Move three spaces. Mathematicians call this finding the digital root.

Object: To score twenty-five points or to capture four disasters, mysteries or famous structures. Owning disasters, structures and mysteries can be accomplished by landing on them in a normal turn, trading for them when you land on a trading post or buying one of them for two times their value when you land on the bank. Children like making the properties on scraps of paper before the game begins for easier exchange and banking. Each time you land on a property, you color in (or initial) the little block in the corner of the property and put the points in your running bank. Ownership will change after trades only. Cross them out on the score sheet and add them to the other column. A scoreboard is provided for you. Each time someone lands on your property, he must pay you the number of points indicated in the top right-hand corner. Each time you land on your own property, you receive twice the points shown.

Winning Sets: Disasters (Chicago Fire, San Francisco Earthquake, Atlantis disappears and *Titanic* sinks); mystery (Loch Ness, Big Foot, Yeti and dinosaurs); structures (Eiffel Tower, Leaning Tower of Pisa, Great Sphinx and Stonehenge)

Player One's Properties/Score	Player Two's Properties/Score

Game Card Property Pieces

On this page are the twelve game pieces for *The Mysteries of Harris Burdick.* Cut them out and place them on oaktag to prolong their usability. Place a little box next to the gameboard as a storage area. Each time someone lands on an appropriate board space, he receives points and one of the game cards to verify property ownership. It also makes property trading much easier. The next time you play the game, design your own game card property pieces. Design a gameboard and create your own educational board game. Pick a theme. Then try to add important facts and intellectual flavor to your game.

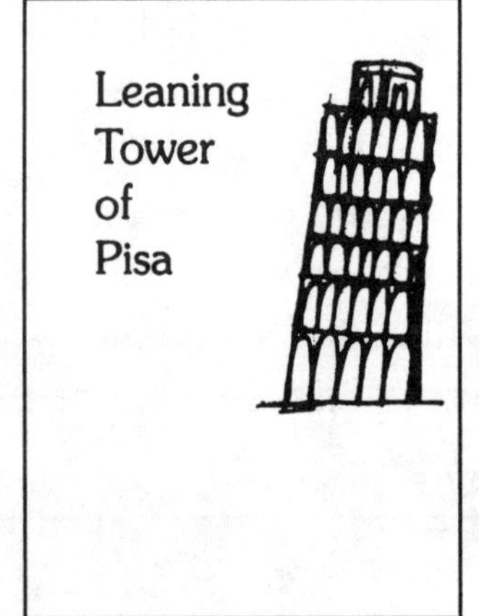

The Unexplained

A Wondrous Adventure

Two Bad Ants

In Search of a Crystal An Ant Expedition

Strange Kitchen Situations Stories to Tell

The Queen's Delight Back in Line

ADVENTURE

Lead-Ins to Literature

How much trouble can two ants get into anyway? Did they leave the protection of the colony? Have they forgotten to hand in their homework assignments? Have they been picking on the spiders and flies in the neighborhood? Did they forget to take out the garbage when Mom told them?

1. What kind of troubles, other than spoiling someone's picnic, could ants get into? ________
2. Most humans think ants are bad. What would another ant think is bad? ________
3. Ants are one of the strongest creatures in the world. They can pick up fifty times their own body weight. Humans can pick up $2^1/_2$ times their own body weight. What other facts do you know about ants? ________
4. In what setting do you think the author will put his ant characters? School? House? Yard? Anthill? Glass terrarium? Forest? Cave? ________
5. If you were drawing the ants, how would you dress them? Would you use clothes like we wear, or would you put them in special outfits? Please explain. ________
6. Would you make your ants male, female or both? Would they be young in age and characteristics or two older-type characters? My class voted that they be neither male nor female? How would this change their story? ________
7. Would you give the ants the same types of problems that kids in the classroom have, or would you give them problems that will make kids think when they read about them? ________
8. Many books have animals that communicate with children. How would you weave a story where ants talk to children? ________
9. What other insects would you place in an ant story? Why? ________
10. Ants feed on many insects and keep the insect population down. They eat mold from leaves and carry seeds from place to place. What other ways are ants helpful? Would you place educational facts like these in a story setting for *Two Bad Ants*? Aliki in *Digging Up Dinosaurs* uses this type of storytelling information approach. ________

Just the Facts

1. Who presented the crystal to the ant queen? ______________________
2. Whose happiness made the ant nest a happy place? ______________________
3. How was the journey to the crystals described? ______________________
4. For whom did the ants anxiously listen? ______________________
5. What did the wind bend? ______________________
6. In the strange new world that the ants found on their journey, what were the first three things that they found were missing? ______________________
7. The wall they followed the scout up was smooth and ______________________.
8. How did the ants feel in this unnatural place? ______________________
9. What did the ants do when they were too full to move? ______________________
10. What color was the scoop that shoveled up the two bad ants and the crystals? ____________
11. What two words described the lake that the ants were thrown into? ____________
12. What was created by the spinning scoop? ______________________
13. The lake was tilted and emptied into a ______________________.
14. A strange red glow caused the ______________________ to rise.
15. The disk the ants were on seemed to ______________________ through the air.
16. After leaving the drink, what did the ants seem to be using for a hiding space? ____________
17. What was pouring from the silver tube? ______________________
18. In what condition was the fruit that the ants fell into? ______________________
19. How was the force described that passed through the wet ants? ____________

What Is Your Opinion?

1. What ideas on the cover of this book would attract people to read the story? What would you change on the cover to attract more people to the plight of two ants? ______________

2. What is your opinion about ants/people who work all their lives just to make the queen bee happy? ______________

3. When you heard the ant scout talk about the location of a crystal, what did you predict the crystal was? ______________

4. In ant terms, how far do you think a long, dangerous journey would be? ______________

5. Did you think the two ants were bad or just curious? Please explain. ______________

6. At first I thought the mystery crystal was salt. What convinced you that it wasn't salt? ______________

7. What places in the book did you recognize by their drawings? Did you know the forest was just parts of a lawn and that the mountain was a side of a house or building? ______________

8. If two members of a small scouting party were missing, wouldn't you be aware of this fact? What are some reasons the ants wouldn't be missed? ______________

9. The ants seem to be stuck in a family breakfast. What was the most creatively presented idea of the breakfast? ______________

10. Would you consider the ants resourceful or just lucky to survive all their new encounters? ______________

11. Did you think at any point in the story that the ants were going to be discovered by humans? ______________

12. What was the author trying to teach? ______________

13. Did you think being shot out of a light socket was funny, or did you think the author carried it a little bit too far when he tried to electrocute the two ants? ______________

Vexing Vocabulary

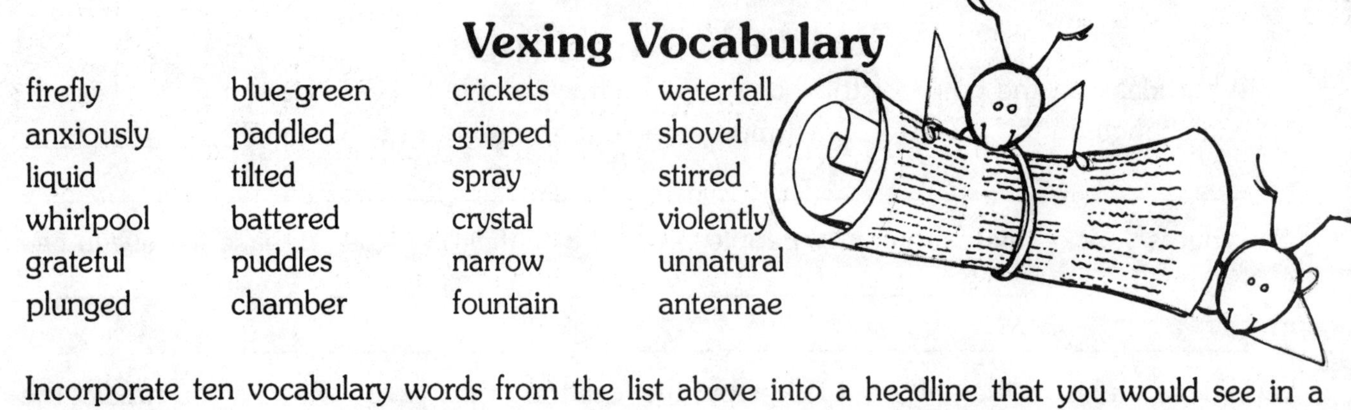

firefly	blue-green	crickets	waterfall
anxiously	paddled	gripped	shovel
liquid	tilted	spray	stirred
whirlpool	battered	crystal	violently
grateful	puddles	narrow	unnatural
plunged	chamber	fountain	antennae

Incorporate ten vocabulary words from the list above into a headline that you would see in a newspaper. Then write the first two lines (lead-in) of the story using another word from the vocabulary list above. Write your best headline on $8^1/_2$" x 11" (21.6 x 27.94 cm) art paper and illustrate the story lead-in. Make your headline/lead-in and your classmates' into a mural.

Example:
Words to be used (shovel, fountain)
Headline–Trevi *Fountain* Destroyed
Lead-in sentences–The famed Trevi fountain is no more. Late last night a runaway steam *shovel*, owned by the Midal Corporation, destroyed the famous tourist attraction.

Words to be used (crystal, liquid)
Headline ______________________________
Lead-in sentences ______________________________

Words to be used (spray, firefly)
Headline ______________________________
Lead-in sentences ______________________________

Words to be used (unnatural, whirlpool)
Headline ______________________________
Lead-in sentences ______________________________

Words to be used (antennae, battered)
Headline ______________________________
Lead-in sentences ______________________________

Words to be used (crickets, spray)
Headline ______________________________
Lead-in sentences ______________________________

Words to be used (tilted, blue-green)
Headline ______________________________
Lead-in sentences ______________________________

Anthill Revisited

Drills for Skills

It is time to try to solve these "ant word" clues, my little picnic pests. Each clue will help you find a word that has *ant* in it in exact order. Evaluate your answer and place the number of consonants in your word over the total letters in the word. Use the back of this page to see if you can find additional "ant words" to add to this activity. Color in half an ant for each answer you solve correctly.

Clue	Answer	Fraction
Example: a deer's horns	antlers	5/7
1. a contraction	______________	______________
2. 100-year-old artifacts	______________	______________
3. small insect devourer	______________	______________
4. a cactus ______________	______________	______________
5. Paul Revere's light	______________	______________
6. Christmas hero	______________	______________
7. car radiator protector	______________	______________
8. African deer	______________	______________
9. an ocean	______________	______________
10. a national song	______________	______________
11. a Civil War general	______________	______________
12. leg covers	______________	______________
13. peanut brand name	______________	______________
14. camping water holder	______________	______________
15. have-to-have word	______________	______________
16. New Mexico capital	______________	______________
17. a baby's crying fit	______________	______________
18. extra large person	______________	______________
19. Indian burial song/prayer	______________	______________
20. lost island	______________	______________

Ideas and Illustrations

The habitats of ants are as interesting as they are varied. Below you will find an anthill, ant farm (on a child's table), a below-ground ant colony and an ant nest weaved like a spider would weave her nest. The scenes are partially drawn for you. After researching the appearance of each location, complete each picture with the added features necessary. Place the source for information about each of your drawings below the drawing.

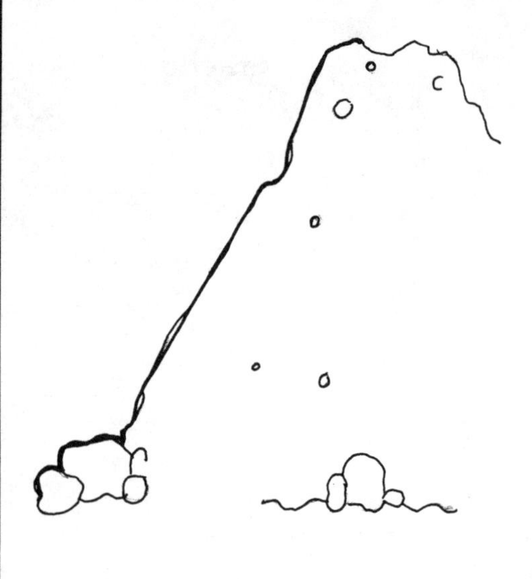

1. Source one ______________________________

2. Source two ______________________________

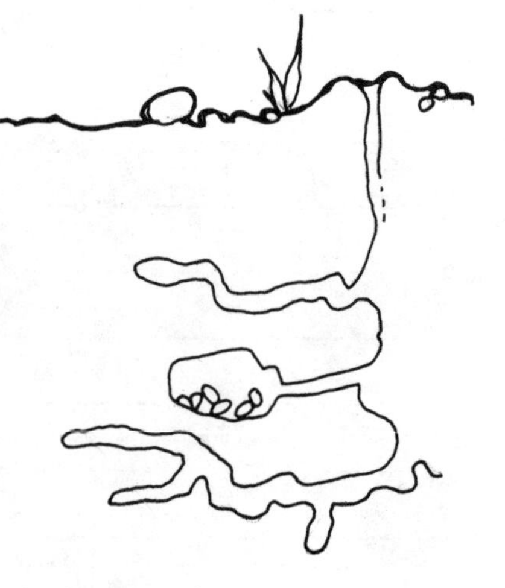

3. Source three ______________________________

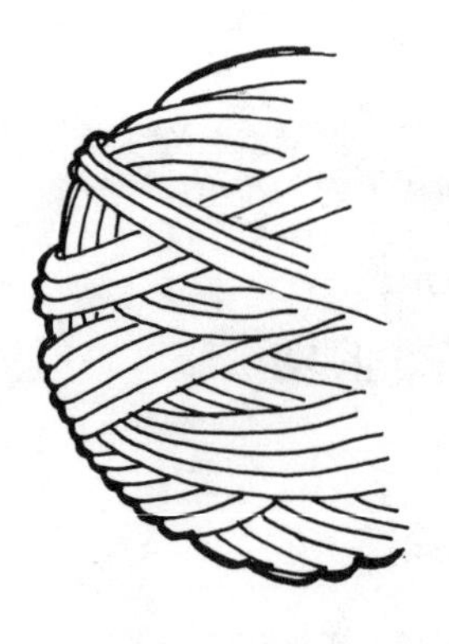

4. Source four ______________________________

1. source one ______________________________
2. source two ______________________________
3. source three ______________________________
4. source four ______________________________

Short-Term Project

There is a wealth of topics that can be researched in the study of insects and ants in particular. Write a short note indicating the research you have found on each topic listed below.

a. ant body parts ______________________________

b. ant communication ______________________________

c. ant reproduction ______________________________

d. the three classes of ants ______________________________

e. the ant social system ______________________________

f. ant species ______________________________

g. life span ______________________________

h. construction techniques ______________________________

i. the queen ______________________________

j. the workers ______________________________

k. the males ______________________________

l. red ants ______________________________

m. flying capabilities ______________________________

n. the soldier ant ______________________________

o. ant legends/fables ______________________________

Select three of your best research topics. Place them on 11" x 14" (27.94 x 35.56 cm) paper. Include a creative title, descriptive illustrations, charts and graphs with your research items.

Research Suggestions

1. Make a parallel comparison chart. This is created by taking an ant characteristic and finding some other creature that has the same trait. The object is not to find one creature that has many of the ant's characteristics. Instead, you are trying to find many creatures that have at least one thing in common with the ant. Pick ten characteristics of the ant. Under each characteristic try to find one or more creatures who may exhibit the same habits or features. (Example 1: travels great distances in search of food...bee...wolf...hawk...) (Example 2 great sense of smell...bee...social insects...snake...dog.) This makes a great chart idea. Each classmate can pick a creature of his own. Computer-generated pictures really enhance this type of project.
2. Our class makes "Vote for ______________ (animal or insect or other idea)" posters for king of the jungle. Author's note: One of my students made a "Vote for my sister as king of the jungle, because she screams louder, bites harder, eats more, etc., than any animal." Why not make posters for what insect should be king/queen of the insect world. Make an insect poster humorous and another serious in your approach for selecting them.
3. Design a movie poster advertising Walt Disney's new movie *Two Bad Ants*. Your classmates may want to design movie posters for their favorite books.
4. Find out what an entomologist is. Research the type of schooling that is needed to become an entomologist. Investigate your area to see what type of job opportunities are available to someone who wants to work with insects. Design a job opportunity flyer for someone advertising for an assistant in some field of insect work.
5. Imagine that you own an aviary and are responsible for finding insect populations for feeding the birds in your zoo. Make an illustrated chart showing the bird on the left and the type of insects it eats on the right. Discuss with your classmates the food chain linkage between the bird, insect and plant world.
6. Write a "Don't kill the ant speech" (or insect of your choice) detailing why the ant/choice of insect should be preserved.
7. Design an insect calendar using your illustrations, drawings and cutout pictures to highlight an insect for each month. Then make a humorous insect month by taking one month and designing made-up holidays and special occasions pertaining to insects. (Example: September 3, DDT banned in the United States; September 11, Kermit the Frog becomes a vegetarian; September 19, National Praying Mantis Day)

Teacher Suggestions

1. The Tell Me Why series tape *Insects* is a good start for introducing *Two Bad Ants*. The last topic is ants. For the older grades, the National Geographic tape on *The Invisible World* is a good follow-up for discussions on small things. If you need a good film on how the food chain works and how an animal study is conducted, the National Geographic film *Alligators* does an excellent job in this area. These movies are available at your local video store. Our school received a math/science grant and purchased the fourteen films of the Tell Me Why series and ten films in the National Geographic series. Award-winning literature videos to correspond to our great books program like *The Lion, the Witch and the Wardrobe* and *The Phantom Tollbooth* were also purchased. In the book *Integrating the Literature of Judy Blume in the Classroom* (pages 32-34), organizing a walkathon for books is discussed. The same walkathon organization can be used to obtain videos or computers for your school.
2. Children's Writing and Publishing Center, a program by the Learning Company, is a must for your computer laboratory. It has changed a school of reluctant writers to a school of infinitely creative authors, truly amazing! It is an easy-to-use word processor with a wealth of easy-to-use graphics. It is excellent for story writing, newspaper development and letter writing lessons.
3. Discuss insect survival and their capabilities of adapting to various situations with your class. Show how these characteristics have allowed some species to exist for thousands of years. Follow this with a life cycle chart of five of the most common insects in your area.
4. Make an Insects and Disease poster with your students highlighting various insects and the diseases they carry and cause. Discuss prevention methods and write to the National Disease Control Center in Atlanta or a local center in your area requesting information about local insects and their disease-carrying characteristics. Form mini groups with your class to research sleeping sickness, typhoid, cholera, dysentery, "the Black Death" and others.
5. Have your class design and conduct a campaign for king and queen of the insect world. My classes designed posters and wrote TV and radio spots and nominating speeches for their insect selections. They also created strange insects of their own. My favorite was a Mike-ider. The child pasted his head on that of a black widow spider and made up characteristics paralleling a spider and human. Have each child use his school picture combined with an insect's body.
6. Have a Lego, toothpick and pipe cleaner insect creating contest.
7. Have your class create *Insect News,* a program designed for insects by insects. The news should include food, recreation and travel ideas.
8. Have your class design a fast-food eatery for insects and create ten food choices that might be served there.

Tell Me Why

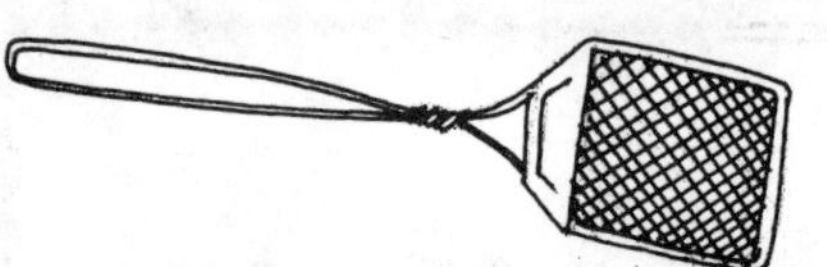

Write Like a Master

The theme for these story starters is the creative use of an insect in an insect story or a story that normally wouldn't include insects. Try to visualize yourself in different situations. This will help you to write predictable and unpredictable formats for each story starter below.

Story Starter I

"Alice, can you come here for a minute? Did you leave the honey someplace last night? Was the cap tightly sealed or was it open? If it was tightly sealed, then I think we may have a giant problem." Yes, we have a giant problem. Look at this ____________________

____

____

____

____

Story Starter II

(Telephone call format) Bug Busters. This is Terry Terminator, the ghostbuster of bug control. How can I help you, Madam? Yes, we accept all credit cards. Yes, Visa is included. Calm down, Ma'am, and explain your problem. We've handled every problem imaginable. I take that back, Madam. I never have seen an insect that large. It's doing what? ____________________

____

____

____

____

____

Story Starter III

My ant research is sure to win first prize at the science fair. It will knock the judges' socks off. I will probably have to be on TV once they see my idea. I have my ants ____________________

____

____

____

____

____

Story Starter IV

Everyone knows of the creation of Spiderman. My new female heroine is patterned after the ____________ (select insect), and my new male hero is patterned after a ____________ (select bird). Their powers and characteristics will include ____________________

____

____

They surely will become members of the Superheroes Hall of Fame for the following deeds: ____

____

____

Gameboard

Materials Needed: Two number cubes, movers, light-colored crayons; Vexing Vocabulary; Just the Facts; student-made and teacher-made question cards can be placed in the areas provided for them in the center of the gameboard. They are optional but highly recommended. A card is picked each time a player has a multiple of five points in his/her bank (5, 10, 15, 20 or 25).

Players Needed: Two to four players or teams of two players

Play Procedures: Players alternate turns; throw number cubes; move in either direction at any time. This allows for playing strategies, rather than just mindlessly moving around a gameboard.

The Roll: Roll both number cubes. Your teacher will tell you to conduct some math operations with the number cubes. The three rules used most often in my classroom are

(a) Subtract the smaller from the larger; then move that many spaces (6 - 4 = 2). Move two spaces.

(b) Multiply the two cubes and move the number of spaces in the one's column of the answer (2 x 6 = 12). Move two spaces.

(c) Keep on adding the two cubes until you get one digit as the answer (6 + 6 = 12, 12 = 1 + 2 = 3). Move three spaces. Mathematicians call this finding the digital root.

Object: To score twenty-five points or to capture four diseases, insects or four endangered species. Owning insects and endangered species can be accomplished by landing on them in a normal turn, trading for them when you land on a trading post or buying one of them for two times their value when you land on the bank. Each time you land on a property you color in (or initial) the little block in the corner of the property and put the points in your running bank. Ownership will change after trades only. Cross them out on the score sheet and add them to the other column. A scoreboard is provided for you. Each time someone lands on your property, he must pay you the number of points indicated in the top right-hand corner. Each time you land on your own property, you receive twice the points shown.

Winning Sets: Diseases (sleeping sickness, malaria, yellow fever and typhoid fever); insects (monarch butterfly, honeybee, wasp and black widow spider); endangered species (California condor, whooping crane, manatee and blue whale)

Player One's Properties/Score	Player Two's Properties/Score

Game Card Property Pieces

On this page are the twelve game pieces for *Two Bad Ants.* Cut them out and place them on oaktag to prolong their usability. Place a little box next to the gameboard as a storage area. Each time someone lands on an appropriate board space, he receives points and one of the game cards to verify property ownership. It also makes property trading much easier. The next time you play the game, design your own game card property pieces. Design a gameboard and create your own educational board game. Pick a theme. Then try to add important facts and intellectual flavor to your game.

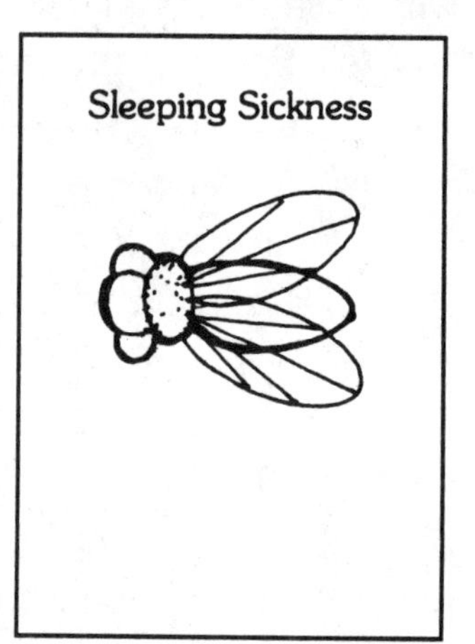

From Dangers to Endangered Species

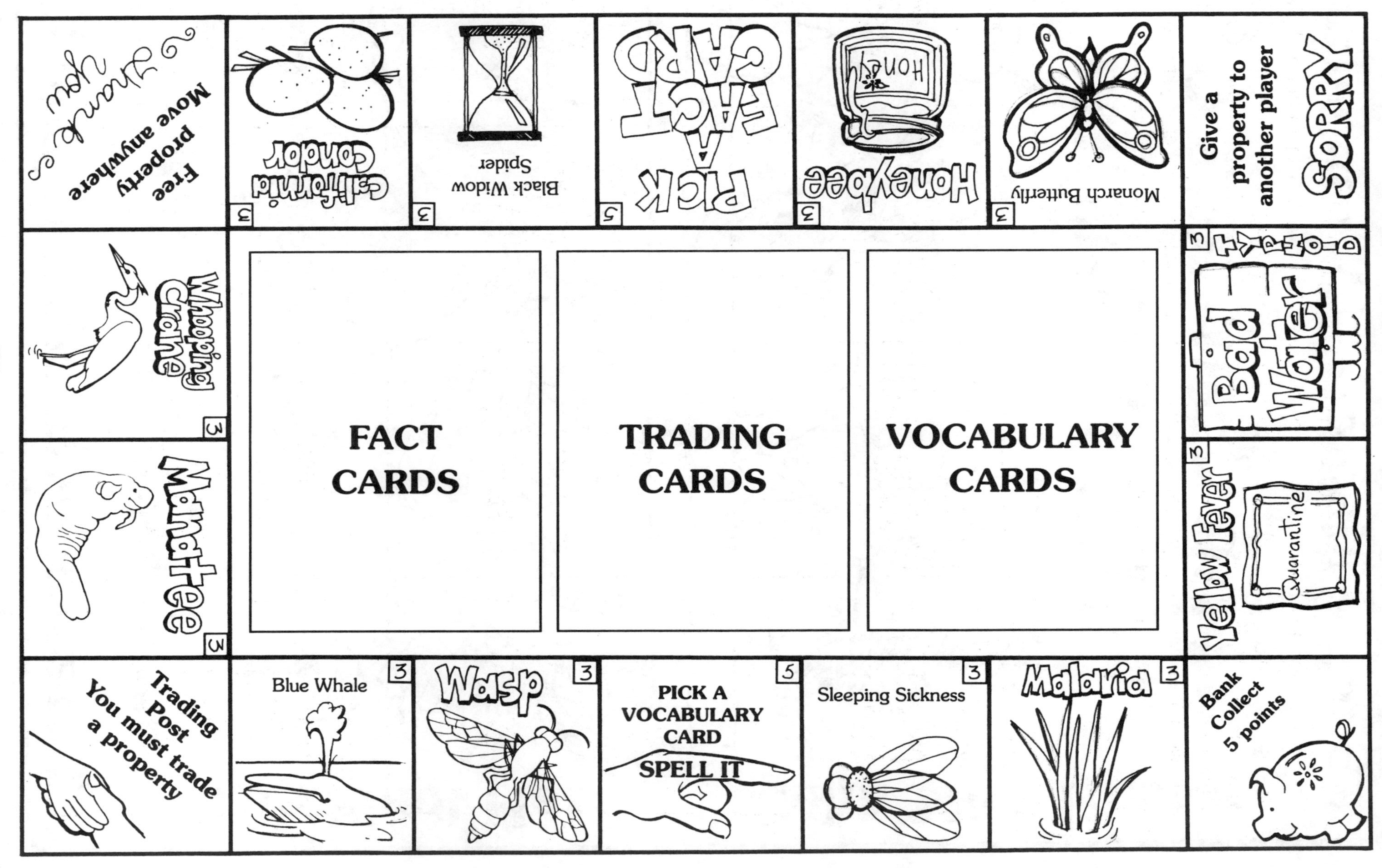

Simple Magic

Wrong Turns

The Garden of Abdul Gasazi

Calm Miss Hester

Fritz the Fast

The Final Hat

Gasazi's Spell

Unbreakable Spells

Flying Dogs

Lead-Ins to Literature

A mysterious garden, a dog-hating magician and a well-meaning boy form the basis for this mystery. Did the magician turn Alan's dog into a duck? How can the spell be broken? Will Alan be allowed to leave Abdul Gasazi's garden after breaking the no-dog rule? Did the mysterious events really happen? Will the danger increase, decrease or continue to affect children that own animals? These questions and some new ones of your own might be answered by reading Chris Van Allsburg's *The Garden of Abdul Gasazi.*

1. Would you watch the troublesome dog of a next-door neighbor? When? What situations would cause you to refuse the watching opportunity? ______________________________
2. Magic is one of the favorite subjects of school-age children. Would you have been fearful of a sign that said beware of the magician? Why? Why not? ______________________________
3. What is your favorite type of dog/magician/bird? Why? ______________________________
4. How would you have titled this book to attract greater attention to it? Do you think the word *garden* adds or takes away from the book's mystery? ______________________________
5. If you were to design a garden in a mystery story, what elements would you put in the story and how would you design your garden?. What features would make your garden original? ______________________________
6. What jobs can you name that would be directly related to gardening and a mysterious garden? ______________________________
7. In most mysteries do you find that more girls, boys or animals end up being lost? What books have you read that focus on a lost girl, boy or animal?
   Lost girl book: ______________________________
   Lost boy book: ______________________________
   Lost animal book: ______________________________
8. Have you ever been lost? When/Where? Briefly describe the experience. ______________________________

Just the Facts

1. What was the name of the dog that Alan was supposed to watch? ____________

2. Who owns Fritz? ____________

3. What did Fritz enjoy chewing on in the living room? ____________

4. What did Alan hide under his shirt? Why?

5. What type of magician did the "absolutely no admittance" sign say that Abdul Gasazi was? ____________

6. Where did the great stairs lead? ____________

7. The door opened before Alan touched the ____________.

8. Who called the dog Fritzie? ____________

9. What were the magician's reasons for detesting dogs? ____________

10. What did Alan follow into the forest? ____________

11. Alan had ____________ in his eyes when he started for home with the dog that now was a duck.

12. What was Alan too old to believe? ____________

13. When Alan climbed the great stairs, what did he think had happened to Fritz? ____________

14. What two words showed that Abdul did not want anyone to bother him? ____________

15. What kind of tug allowed Fritz to detach himself from his dog collar? ____________

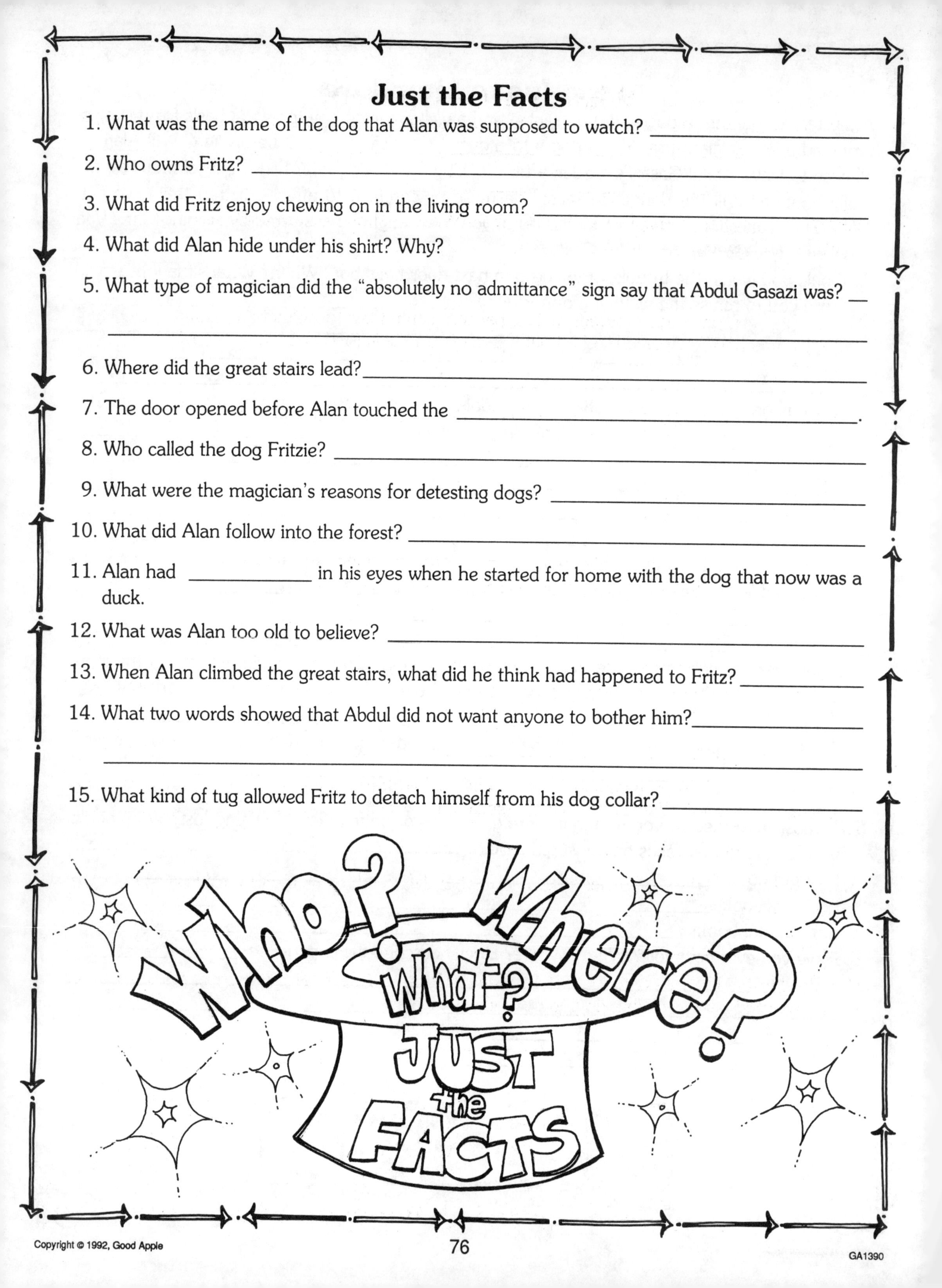

What Is Your Opinion?

1. Don't you think Alan was a bit foolish to go to sleep, if he were responsible for watching someone? ______________________________

2. The dog bit Aunt Eunice six different times. What kind of woman would ask a little boy to watch such a dog? ______________________________

3. Wouldn't you have been curious as to what was behind the "absolutely no admittance" sign? Would you have trespassed to find out if a magician really lived next door to you? ______________________________

4. What made Alan think that he had to find Fritz before Mr. Gasazi found him? ______________________________

5. If you were sure someone in a great mysterious house captured your dog, wouldn't you go for help instead of entering the house on your own? ______________________________

6. A door opening before I even knocked is "out of there" stuff for me. What about you? ______________________________

7. Did you ever yell "look out" to a character in a movie or story you know? Just before the vampire is ready to strike, your mind says "look out." At what part of the story would you have cautioned Alan to "look out" or be careful? ______________________________

8. Chris Van Allsburg's magician seems to be Middle Eastern looking. How would you have made him scarier? Would a woman magician have been just as frightening? How? ______________________________

9. If one of the ducks was turned into a dog, what did you think all the other ducks were before they were ducks? ______________________________

10. Miss Hester lived next to Gasazi for years. Come on now! There must have been other strange happenings. What do you think she is hiding? ______________________________

What Is Your Opinion?

Vexing Vocabulary

Eunice	bizarre	eerie	approached
Abdul	invitation	exhausted	gust
absolutely	positively	magician	forever
certain	convinced	nervously	fellow
shadow	apologized	perhaps	blurted
Fritz	bellowed	midair	promised

Many textbooks describe "said words" as words that identify the manner in which you are speaking. Words included in this category are *whispered, yelled, cried, pleaded, bellowed, blurted* and more. Complete each "said word" sentence below using at least two vocabulary words in your response.

Example: ____, she scolded.
"Fritz, you are a positively awful dog," she scolded.

1. ____, the magician bellowed.
2. ____, she sighed.
3. ____, Aunt Eunice gasped.
4. Miss Hester called, ____.
5. ____, they shouted.
6. Alan screamed, ____.
7. Fritz pleaded, ____.
8. ____, the bully chided.
9. ____, she repeated.
10. The captain warned, ____.
11. Mother always says, ____.
12. The counselor suggested, ____.

Can you find five additional "said words" that were not used in this activity? 1. ____________
2.____________ 3.____________ 4.____________ 5.____________

Why do you think proper use of "said words" will make a potential creative writer a better describer of events and a better storyteller?

A Flower by What Name Did You Say?

Drills for Skills

In one of my earlier books, I wrote clues that would lead to a flower's name. This is the perfect time to upgrade that activity. On the left you will find clues that will generate flower names. Record the flowers on the right. In the second part of the activity, pick a flower's name. Try to write a clue that will allow a person to guess that flower's name. Research your state flower after completing this work sheet.

Clues	**Flower's Name**
This flower is	
1. a vehicle	______________
2. what baked bread did	______________
3. part of your face	______________
4. an upturned dress part	______________
5. the opposite of *night*	______________
6. what people do at a wedding	______________
7. an untruth	______________
8. a boy's name	______________
9. part of the eye	______________
10. cooking utensil	______________
11. is our biggest star	______________
12. *mom*'s opposite	______________
13. Middle Age's monster	______________
14. happy	______________
15. musical notes	______________
16. a funny duck	______________
17. a black watcher bird	______________
18. hits the net in tennis	______________

If you are not a flower expert, ask your teacher to write the flower names on the board before giving the clues.

Famous Magicians, Wizards, Sorcerers and Witches

Short-Term Project I

Pick four of the denizens of magic to report on in the boxes below. Highlight their characteristics, story/role, powers and secret spells. Add a mini illustration with each character. Transfer your drawing and story for each on 11" x 14" (27.94 x 35.56 cm) paper. You and your classmates might want to make a mural titled "Magic Masters of All Ages" with the best illustrations from this project.

- Merlin
- Rumpelstiltskin
- Satan
- Minotaur of Crete
- Cheshire Cat
- King Midas
- Wizard of Speed and Time
- Wicked Witch of the West
- Nostradamus
- Medusa
- Snow White's Witch
- Thor/Oden/Zeus
- Cinderella's Fairy Godmother
- The Sphinx

List some of your favorite wizards and witches that are not included above.

1. ______________________________
2. ______________________________
3. ______________________________
4. ______________________________
5. ______________________________
6. ______________________________

A Wizard	A Witch
Creature	**Book/Historical Character**

Telephone Poetry

Short-Term Project II

A telephone poet is able to write poems using the letters associated with telephone numbers. Each number in your telephone number has three letters next to it. The first of these three letters is the only one that is used. You are to make a ten-line poem using the first letter that is associated with each number. This letter will begin each line in your poem. Using the telephone number 215-322-7046, the poem below corresponds to the first letter represented by each number. If your telephone number has a one or a zero in it, you are free to choose any letter you want to start that line.

A ... A secret wish came to mind
O ... Of helping people and being kind.
J ... Just think of the joy that we can spread
D ... Doing nice things until time for bed.
A ... An army of nice people is what we'll see;
A ... A lot of children joining you and me.
P ... People will love the kindness we do;
R ... Rich we will be in things so true;
G ... Giving of yourself is the clue;
M ... Make my wish, please, your wish, too.

Try recording your poem in the spaces below.

Write your telephone number here. ____________________

Record each letter associated with your number downward on the blanks provided. Try using a challenging rhyme pattern.

Try composing a secret wish poem that describes the things that an army of nice people could do. You do not need your phone number for this activity.

Thinking of Disappearing Flowers

Ideas and Illustrations

A series of games called NIM (*win* rotated 180 degrees) will challenge your flower removal and thinking skills. In NIM 1 you will place the first thirteen letters of the alphabet on a circle of flowers. You will then alternate picking flowers against a partner. The object is to force the player playing against you to pick up the last flower. Each player on his turn may pick up, color in or mark one or two flowers. If two flowers are selected, they must be flowers with consecutive letters. If the letters *A, C* and *F* are left in the game and it is your turn, you are prevented from picking up two letters, in this instance, because the two letters you would have to select to win the game are not consecutive. Use the gameboard below to play a classmate. Place counters on each flower before beginning the game. This way you can play the game again and again without marking up this paper. Play the best out of five games to determine a winner.

After the game is completed, design a thirteen-flower gameboard that you can use the next time you play this game. Try making each flower unique. Maybe you are lucky and your school might have a laminating machine that you can put your game through. This machine puts a protective cover on your work.

Is there a strategy for winning this game, or is it just a game of luck? Should you go first or second to always insure winning? Does the number of flowers in the game make a difference for the winning strategy? What would happen if you could pick three flowers at a time?

Research Suggestions

There are hundreds of interesting ideas that relate to gardens and plants, birds, dogs and magicians. Form a research team, divide up a research theme and put together a final presentation. Some ideas you might want to pursue are listed below.

1. Bird conservationists have moved species of birds away from endangered environments. Can you highlight four birds that have been changed in such a manner? The ringneck pheasant, common to many parts of Pennsylvania, was brought here from Asia.
2. Can you find three characteristics of ducks and their migration habits?
3. Make a mural to scale of "The Birds of North America." You can feature ten birds in a line from smallest to largest with habitat pictures behind them. Like the duck in the story, make a "Ducks of North America" mural stressing their characteristics and sizes, as a more focused alternative.
4. Research the birds in each of the following:
   a. Edgar Allen Poe's "The Raven"
   b. Samuel Coleridge's albatross, "The Rime of the Ancient Mariner"
   c. The Bible's and Noah's land-seeking dove
   d. The swans in "The Ugly Duckling," *The Trumpet of the Swan* or *Summer of the Swans*
   e. The goose in "Jack and the Beanstalk" and "The Golden Goose"
   f. The Phoenix rising from mythical ashes
5. Research modern day magicians, like David Copperfield, and compare their tricks and approach to magic to Houdini's feats.
6. Do you have a botanical garden nearby? That is a specially designed garden where plants are grown chiefly for scientific, educational, environmental, architectural and artistic purposes. If you can't visit one, have your class design ten questions that can be forwarded to the closest botanical garden. Include some of your class research, thoughts, drawings and discoveries with your requests. Most gardens will send you a portfolio of interesting topics.
7. What is the importance of botany (the study of plants)?
8. Research five authors/illustrators, like Lewis Carroll's *Alice in Wonderland,* who also made garden scenes important to their stories.
9. The Hanging Gardens of Babylon are one of the ancient wonders of the world. What made them unique? What modern garden/natural wonders would you compare to them? Why?
10. Holland is noted as the Flower Trade Capital of the World. Stop into your local flower shop and investigate the shipping/growing origins of the flowers that they order. Make a flag/pin map showing where each flower originates.

Teacher Suggestions

1. The first suggestion sounds like something every teacher would do. But we classroom teachers often forget to do the obvious. Later we find out, through a comparison of work, that the children take a simple idea and turn it into a "glorious, I could cry" work. Have your students make two-tiered dioramas. The first tier's title is "The World's Most Exotic Garden" The second tier's title is "The Mysterious Garden of Abdul Gasazi" or "The Mysterious Garden of Mary Smith" (student's name). Have them in mini presentations highlight the two gardens' similarities and differences.

2. Have your class research the Gardens of Versailles, the Royal Botanical Gardens of Kew, England (origin of rubber studies were done there), the Botanical Gardens of Montreal or New York or the Jardin Des Plantes in Paris, France.

3. Invite the owner of a nearby flower shop to discuss local varieties of flowers and their care. Is there a horticultural society near you that provides speakers? Can someone show your class how to make silk flowers, floral displays or windowsill gardens?

4. Create flower trading cards with your class. They are designed the same way baseball cards are designed but have flowers pictured on the fronts and their statistics on the backs.

5. Design a bulletin board titled "The Flowers of Room 205." Each child places his picture in the center of a drawn or cutout flower and then describes the characteristics of himself as a flower–flower found in messy room ... leans to the direction rock and roll music is played ... prefers to wake up to afternoon, rather than morning sunshine, etc.).

6. Have your class investigate medicinal flowers, plants and shrubs. Science Research Associates (SRA) has reading laboratories in most schools that contain follow-up ideas to the information being presented in this mini unit. Topics range from Fossil Plants to Plants We Eat to The Life of a Flowering Plant and Plant Cells.

7. Pennsylvania is the mushroom capital of the world and out of respect for the author of this book's home state, you might want to research edible and inedible mushrooms or these varieties: chanterelle, shaggy mane, milkcaps, hygrophorus, rhodophyllus, St. George's, fly agaric.

8. Research perfumes and flowers with your class. The girls bring in types of perfume and the boys bring in colognes. The class then writes a consumer report article rating the fragrances that were presented in class. Please remind students to bring in the items' prices, so this can be part of the evaluation.

9. Research various artists whose drawing of flowers are part of some of their major works–Van Gogh/sunflowers, Degas/little girl in bonnet, Renoir, Da Vinci, Vermeer. Make a mural of the great masters and their use of flowers in their drawings.

Write Like a Master

The theme for these story starters is the hunt for something lost in a strange and forbidding location. Try to make the reader of your story feel that there is danger, fear and an unknown outcome in the picture you will be painting with your words in each starter below.

Story Starter I

One wrong turn in this cave and we will have a lost dog and a lost rescuer. I hear you, Rocky! That rock didn't move? It's moving and so am I. Which way? ______________________________

____

____

____

____

Story Starter II

The Book of Reverse Magic and its subtitle *Lost Dog, Don't Lose This* caught my eye and imagination. The dwarf was much too powerful for my trickery. Maybe this book could help after all. Chapter 1...How could you be so stupid...they are right on the nose with that one. I only let Jasper ____

____

____

____

____

____

Story Starter III

I am steamed! No second-rate sorceress is going to change my dog into a duck. I'll wizard her right into another dimension, scary laugh and all. Oops, ______________________________

____

____

____

____

____

Story Starter IV

Aunt Bertha, you have to believe me. This canary is your cat. The reverse magician always turns animals into their enemies, so they will know how it feels from the other side. He gave me this secret lotion to restore Nero back to himself. I am either putting on too little or too much. Do you have any ideas? I know you ____

____

____

____

STORY STARTER

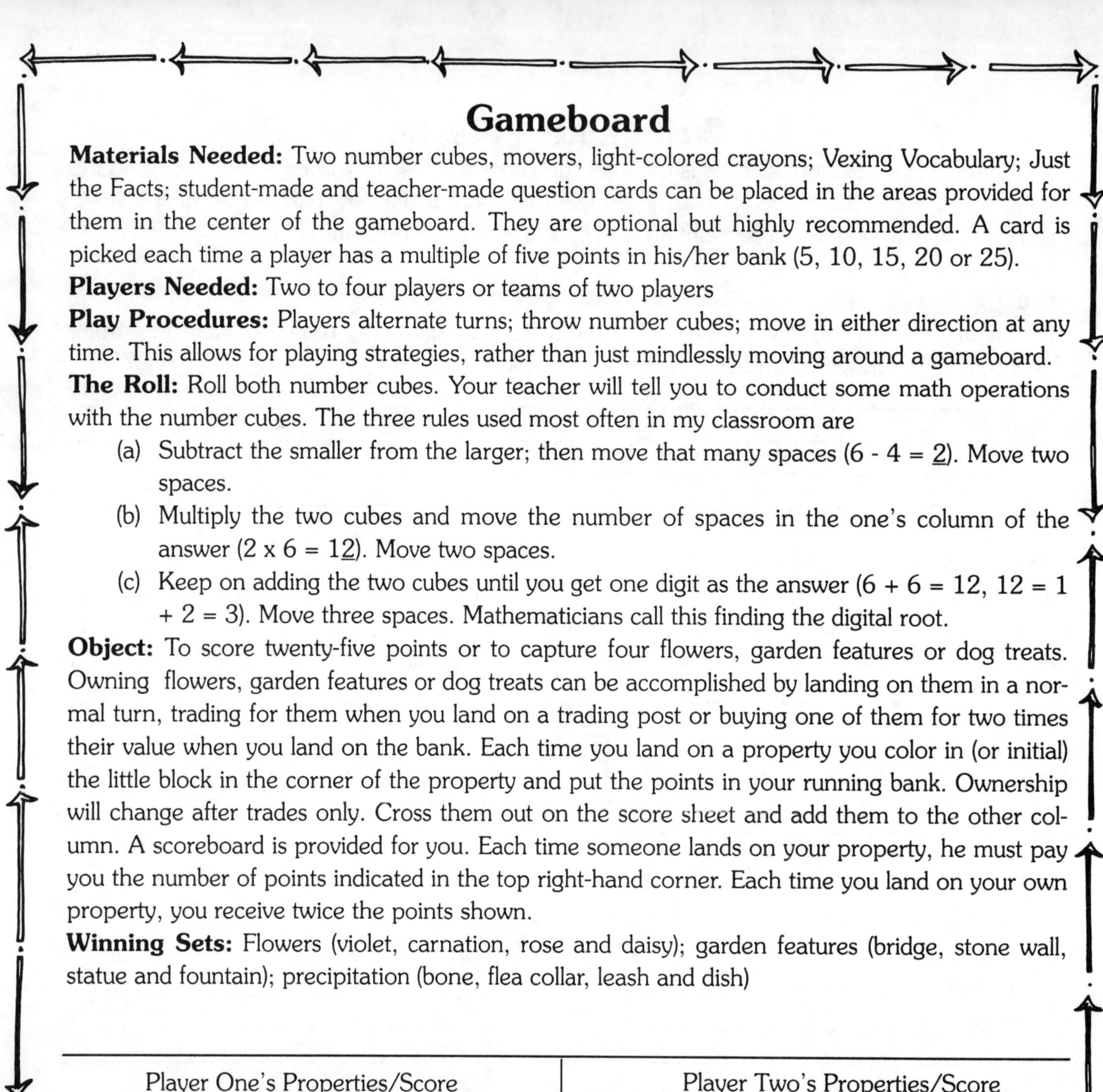

Gameboard

Materials Needed: Two number cubes, movers, light-colored crayons; Vexing Vocabulary; Just the Facts; student-made and teacher-made question cards can be placed in the areas provided for them in the center of the gameboard. They are optional but highly recommended. A card is picked each time a player has a multiple of five points in his/her bank (5, 10, 15, 20 or 25).

Players Needed: Two to four players or teams of two players

Play Procedures: Players alternate turns; throw number cubes; move in either direction at any time. This allows for playing strategies, rather than just mindlessly moving around a gameboard.

The Roll: Roll both number cubes. Your teacher will tell you to conduct some math operations with the number cubes. The three rules used most often in my classroom are

(a) Subtract the smaller from the larger; then move that many spaces (6 - 4 = 2). Move two spaces.

(b) Multiply the two cubes and move the number of spaces in the one's column of the answer (2 x 6 = 12). Move two spaces.

(c) Keep on adding the two cubes until you get one digit as the answer (6 + 6 = 12, 12 = 1 + 2 = 3). Move three spaces. Mathematicians call this finding the digital root.

Object: To score twenty-five points or to capture four flowers, garden features or dog treats. Owning flowers, garden features or dog treats can be accomplished by landing on them in a normal turn, trading for them when you land on a trading post or buying one of them for two times their value when you land on the bank. Each time you land on a property you color in (or initial) the little block in the corner of the property and put the points in your running bank. Ownership will change after trades only. Cross them out on the score sheet and add them to the other column. A scoreboard is provided for you. Each time someone lands on your property, he must pay you the number of points indicated in the top right-hand corner. Each time you land on your own property, you receive twice the points shown.

Winning Sets: Flowers (violet, carnation, rose and daisy); garden features (bridge, stone wall, statue and fountain); precipitation (bone, flea collar, leash and dish)

Player One's Properties/Score	Player Two's Properties/Score

Game Card Property Pieces

On this page are the twelve game pieces for *The Garden of Abdul Gasazi*. Cut them out and place them on oaktag to prolong their usability. Place a little box next to the gameboard as a storage area. Each time someone lands on an appropriate board space, he receives points and one of the game cards to verify property ownership. It also makes property trading much easier. The next time you play the game, design your own game card property pieces. Design a gameboard and create your own educational board game. Pick a theme. Then try to add important facts and intellectual flavor to your game.

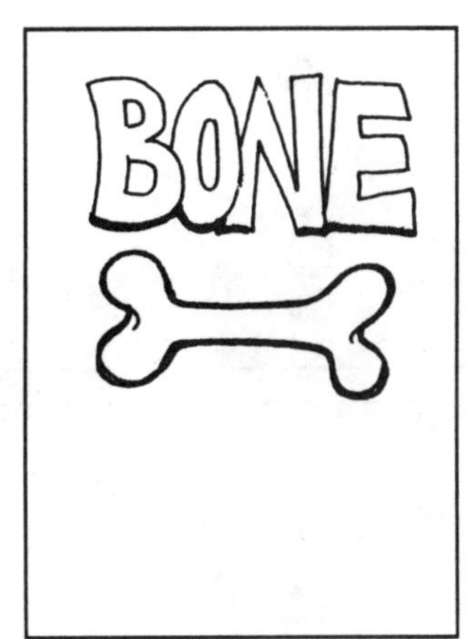

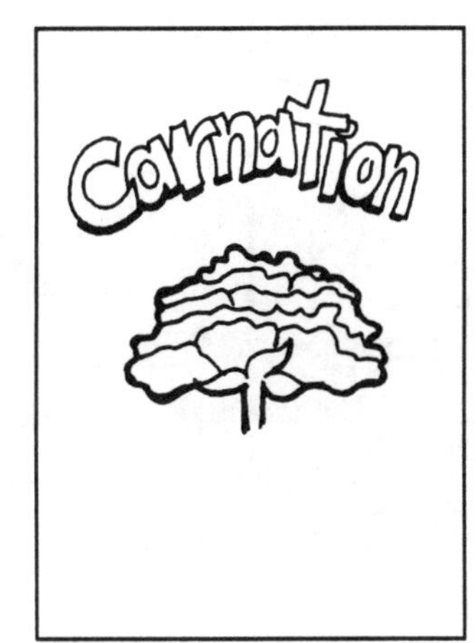

From Flowers to Fleas

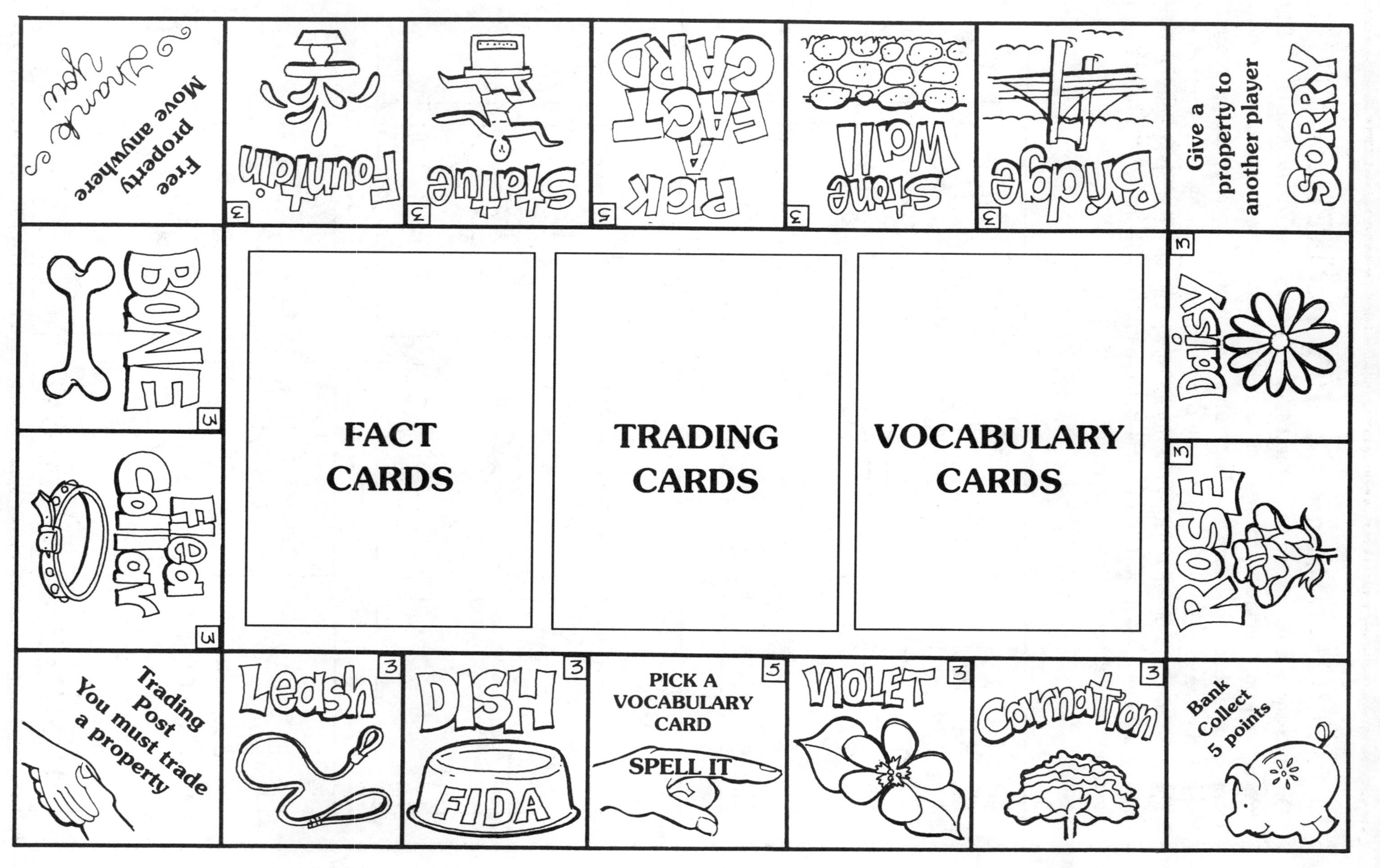

Robots

My Own Airplane

Save Our Environment

Just a Dream

Litter/Smog/Pollution

Time Warp

Tree Planting

Fishless Ocean

Travel by Bed

Lead-Ins to Literature

Have you ever been pulled into a time warp or another dimension? Did you ever have one of your dreams turn ino the world's worst nightmare? Walter the litterbug, an unconcerned citizen, seems to have just this type of problem. His special dreams of the future are destroyed as he and his bed are transported ahead in time. There he sees the problems that he may have caused years before by not caring for or about the environment.

1. Describe what you predict our worst picture of the future would look like? What things are we doing incorrectly now that will cause this to happen?____________________

2. Walter is an "environmental slob." What types of "environment trashing" do you think he is noted for in the story?____________________

3. In the story Walter is transported into the future while sitting on his bed. He then is transported from place to place using his bed. Do you think the author sees the bed as a safe place, even though his lead character is in a strange, threatening territory? Why would a creative writer choose to have his lead character travel by bed?____________________

4. Did you ever have the same dream repeat itself? Explain. ____________________

5. What were the best and worst dreams that you ever had? ____________________

6. Do you think you can control your mind enough to plan what you are going to dream about each night? Why? Why not? ____________________

7. Are our environmental problems really solvable? Explain. ____________________

8. Do you know the differences between a natural and human resource? What are they?__________

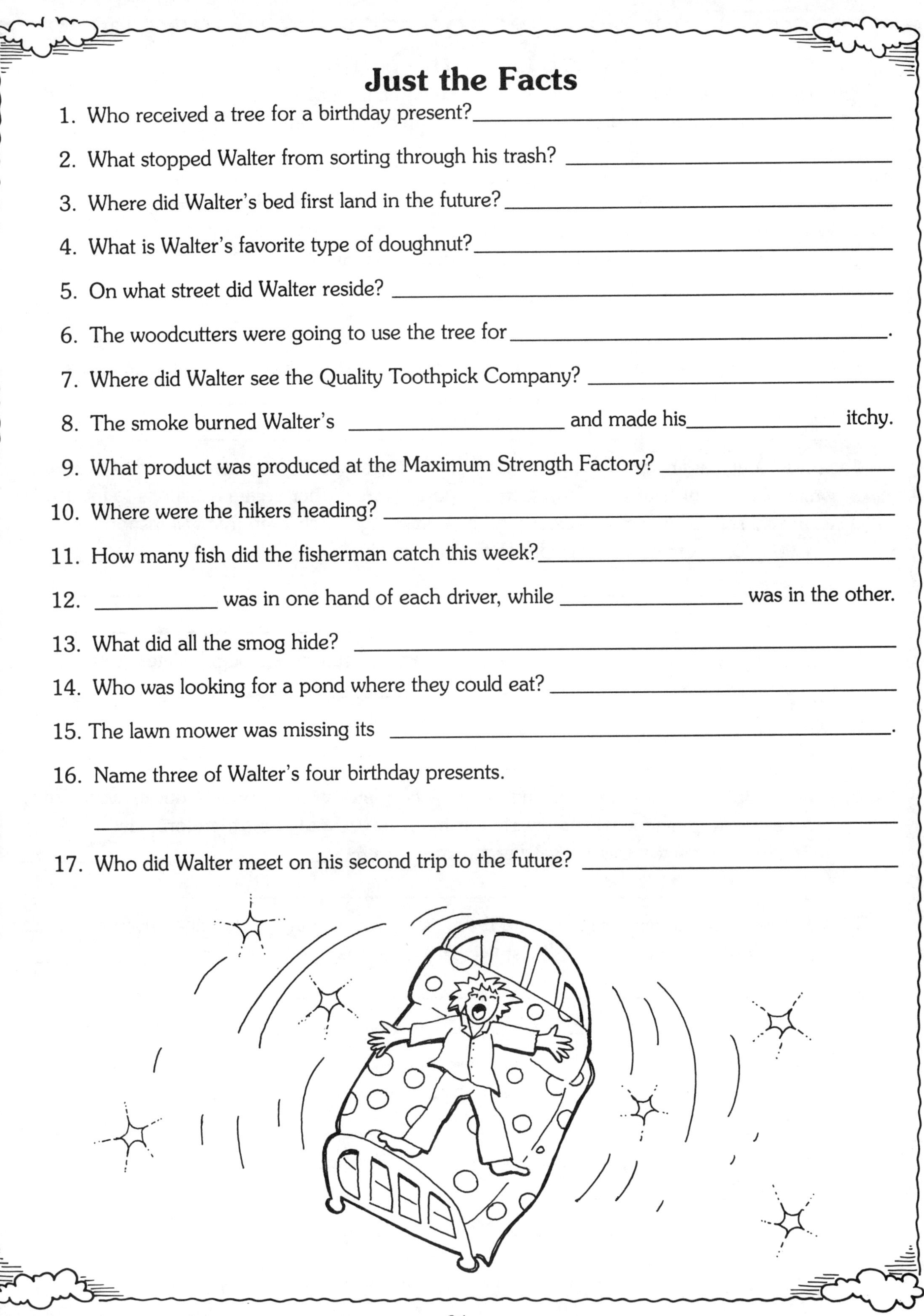

Just the Facts

1. Who received a tree for a birthday present? ____________________
2. What stopped Walter from sorting through his trash? ____________________
3. Where did Walter's bed first land in the future? ____________________
4. What is Walter's favorite type of doughnut? ____________________
5. On what street did Walter reside? ____________________
6. The woodcutters were going to use the tree for ____________________.
7. Where did Walter see the Quality Toothpick Company? ____________________
8. The smoke burned Walter's ______________ and made his ______________ itchy.
9. What product was produced at the Maximum Strength Factory? ____________________
10. Where were the hikers heading? ____________________
11. How many fish did the fisherman catch this week? ____________________
12. ____________ was in one hand of each driver, while ______________ was in the other.
13. What did all the smog hide? ____________________
14. Who was looking for a pond where they could eat? ____________________
15. The lawn mower was missing its ____________________.
16. Name three of Walter's four birthday presents.

    ______________ ______________ ______________

17. Who did Walter meet on his second trip to the future? ____________________

What Is Your Opinion?

1. Do you think that it is possible to see the future in a dream? Aren't a majority of our predictions about the future sort of mental dreams or even daydreams?

2. What three environmental problems will have the greatest effect on future generations? Describe what you think is our greatest environmental problem.

3. In *The Lorax*, Dr. Seuss tells a similar environmental story. How would you compare it to *Just a Dream*?

4. Survey your classmates to see how many dream in color and how many dream in black and white. Write your findings below. Can you design three other dream questions to include in your mini survey? Make a prediction of the percentage of children that will respond to each question. Compare your predictions to the final results.

5. Do you think a dream like the one in the story could cure a litterbug/polluter? What other events might lead to such a person's cure?

6. Many people say that strengthening our pollution laws will put people out of work. They say that cleanup money will be diverted from employees' salaries; therefore, layoffs will be necessary. Do you feel this is a valid argument?

7. What would be the repercussions of a drastic step like banning all gasoline-driven cars from the center of all towns and cities? List five pros and cons of this decision.

8. What do you think about a greenhouse law that says all houses must have green shrubs or two trees in front?

9. What events in the story are most likely to happen? Which events do we stand a chance of preventing?

Vexing Vocabulary

pastry	garbage	beneath	itchy
moment	gazed	replied	coughing
laundry	inflatable	hydrant	drifting
shrieking	Mount Everest	medicine	Grand Canyon
belched	quality	floral	haze
bulging	doughnuts	bulldozer	laser

Incorporate two of the words above in a couplet. Try to place a vocabulary word on each line of the couplet. The vocabulary words do not have to be at the end of a line. See if you can compose three couplets following these rules in the spaces provided.

Examples:
It is impossible to star gaze
Through a wet and misty haze.

Pastry is my favorite treat.
I also think doughnuts can't be beat.

DOUGHNUTS CAN'T BE BEAT!

a. ____________________
a. ____________________

b. ____________________
b. ____________________

c. ____________________
c. ____________________

Try blending this story's vocabulary words into a tercet or quatrain. It is very difficult to put a vocabulary word on each line. Score one point for each line that uses a vocabulary word. Two-vocabulary-word lines get two points.

A shrieking lady yelled,	(one point)
"Where's my inflatable cat?"	(one point)
A woman replied,	(one point)
"He's beneath my floral hat."	(two points)

total points: 5

a. ____________________
b. ____________________
c. ____________________
d. ____________________

Can you incorporate your vocabulary words into a haiku, tanka, prose or other poetic form?

Drills for Skills

In the area of recreational linguistics, there is a type of word that when a certain letter is removed, and the rest of the letters are pushed together, a new word is formed. This type of word is generally called a removal and most frequently has its first or last letters crossed out. No matter what is crossed out, though, it still remains a word. The activity below will give you hints for words that lose their first, last or medial letters. Place the answer to the first clue in column one and the second answer with a letter crossed out in column two. Letters may not be rearranged.

What removals will satisfy these clues?

Example: two babies/scores a victory **twins/wins**

1. between mountains/bowling lane ________ / ________
2. hot vapor/plant part ________ / ________
3. opposite of *sit*/boy's name ________ / ________
4. no cost/a cost ________ / ________
5. very dry/remove ________ / ________
6. a number/not odd ________ / ________
7. go together/arithmetic ________ / ________
8. car accident/skin itch ________ / ________
9. hand warmer/hate's enemy ________ / ________
10. shopping place/open wound ________ / ________
11. chop in half/spew saliva ________ / ________
12. tooth ________/lower than good ________ / ________
13. garden greenery/trousers ________ / ________
14. not closed/writing tool ________ / ________
15. machine of war/color ________ / ________

Use the lines below to create five removals of your own.

________ ________ / ________

________ ________ / ________

________ ________ / ________

________ ________ / ________

________ ________ / ________

Comic Strip-like Art

Ideas and Illustrations

You will find four four-part dream strips provided below.The first scene has been drawn for you in each strip. You are to complete the next three panels in some kind of logical sequence from the first panel. The second panel must have some item in it from the first panel. The third must have some item in it from the second and so on. Cut out each individual strip. Place your impressions from each strip next to your classmates' in poster format.

The four themes for the strips are

1. Person in bed dreaming of space travel
2. Fisherman in boat in polluted waters
3. Trash-filled porch and yard
4. Children climbing mountain with hotel on top

You might want to draw these strips on larger pieces of paper to make your final combination of strips even more impressive.

Space Travel

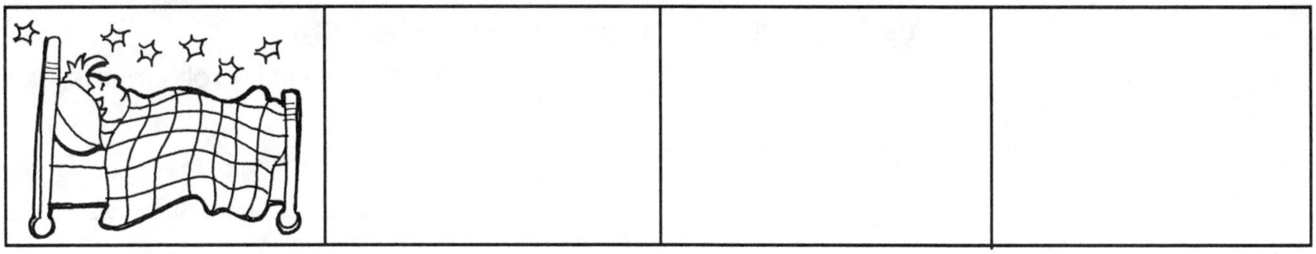

Pollution

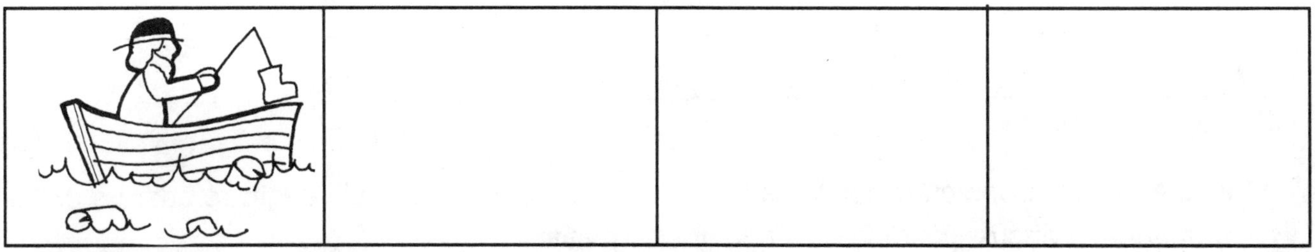

Trash Problem

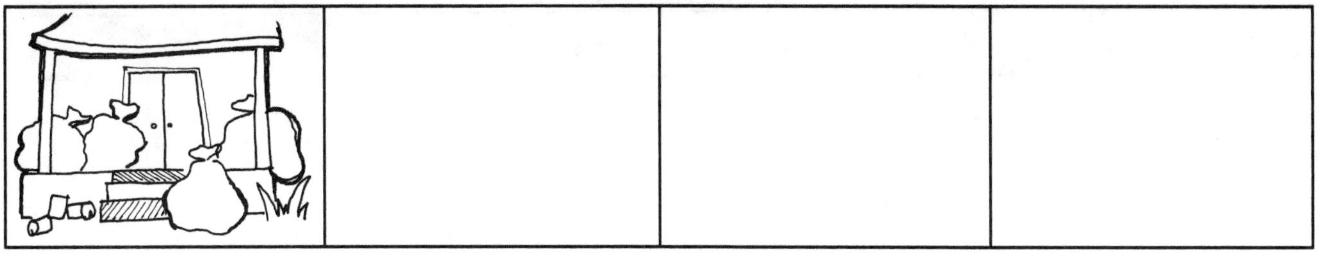

Mountain Hotel

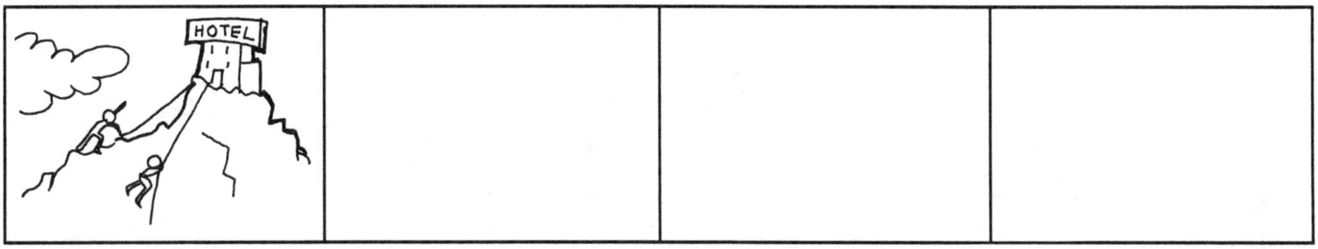

The Environmental Club

Short-Term Project

More and more authors are expressing in their writings the environmental concerns that we all have. The Earth Day Movement, Greenpeace and others have given us a new awareness of problems that will have an impact on all of us. To support this environmental awareness movement, we are suggesting that classes form Save Our Environment clubs. Each club should focus on those easy-to-change problem areas at home, in school and throughout our communities. Membership in the club like membership in our Have an Extra Nice Day Club (appears in *Integrating the Literature of Judy Blume in the Classroom*) is simple. First, you have to design a button that focuses on some problem you'd like to correct or lessen. The button should contain illustrations and a club motto. You then are encouraged to make five recorded contacts of people who will help you by planting trees, conserving water, correcting a problem or lessening one. Please use the form below. Lastly, you will design an environmental poster with suggestions for students and teachers on how they can help save our environment. Share your experiences with your classmates. Remember you will have just as many successes as failures in your undertakings, so don't be discouraged.

Let's Help Our Environment Recording Form

Person's name	task performed/problem lessened
1. ______________________	______________________
2. ______________________	______________________
3. ______________________	______________________
4. ______________________	______________________
5. ______________________	______________________

List the five environmental concerns that you think your club should begin to address or attack. Compare and discuss your ideas with your classmates.

1. ____
2. ____
3. ____
4. ____
5. ____

Save Our Environment Club

The World's Most Famous Inns and Hotels

Short-Term Project II

The hotel on top of Mt. Everest in this story has to be a construction marvel. How and why do you think it was built? What do you know of hotels and hotel chains throughout the world? What type of research information can you find out about hotels or inns in your area and around the world? After reading about a number of hotels, complete the chart below. Pick a hotel that you think is the best of the best, and highlight the hotel in an advertising poster.

Inns/hotels in your area

Hotel	Exact Location	No. Rooms	Comments

Inns/hotels in your state

Hotel	Exact Location	No. Rooms	Comments

Three best inns/hotels in the United States

Hotel	Exact Location	No. Rooms	Comments

Three best inns/hotels outside of the United States

Hotel	Exact Location	No. Rooms	Comments

Place this activity on larger paper and enhance your selections with actual cutout pictures of your hotel choices.

Research Suggestions

1. Write a scenario of what your world will look like when you are twenty-five and fifty years old.
2. Research acid rain. Collect information from three different sources. Compare and contrast the effects of acid rain on European, United States and South American forests and streams.
3. Research auto emissions. What amount of pollutants does an automobile engine throw into the air? How are these pollutants measured? What five cars have the best record for curbing pollutants? What five cars have the worst record?
4. Write a letter to *Consumer Report* for information on a certain environmental test or report.
5. Write the Environmental Protection Agency for information they distribute to classes and school groups on how we can better protect our environment.
6. Have your class organize a park pick-up day. Select a site in your area and recruit volunteers to help clean the area. It is a simple idea that always works for everyone's benefit.
7. Write a poem expressing your concern for our natural resources. Have a classmate illustrate each stanza.
8. Research Ralph Nader or a local consumer protection agency. How many national or local environmental groups can you name? What are some of their membership responsibilities?
9. Design two "before and after" drawings to dramatize the effects of polluting our environment.
10. Assume you are a local or national politician. Write an ecology speech stating your stand on environmental problems and concerns.
11. Can you find three magazines that stress environmental concerns? Cut out two of their articles and share them with your classmates.
12. Design a wall painting showing a civilization that was destroyed by a lack of conservational concern in any area.
13. Write a poem called "Follow Me by Planting a Tree."
14. Design a truck that comes to houses to teach people how to conserve energy. Research the computer game Energy House for use in your classroom program.

Teacher Suggestions

1. Invite a speaker from the weather service, park service, water commission or local environmental group to discuss the safety of our drinking water, rivers, ponds and streams.
2. Show the film *The Vanishing Wilderness* and update some of the points the original writer/narrator was trying to develop.
3. Design a hotel room with your class that would be ideal for children.
4. Start a paper recycling campaign in your classroom. Place all the white paper generated in a garbage bag each week. We use actual recycling (large) boxes in each of our classrooms. Do this for four weeks. Weigh and record the amount of paper collected each week. Take this number and multiply it by twelve for the twelve months of the year. You can see that there are four or five mini lessons in this suggestion already. Then take this number and multiply it by the number of classrooms in the school. Continuous addition can be used if your class can't multiply. Then multiply this number by the number of schools in your community. We have over two hundred schools in Philadelphia. Maybe your class would like to use this number in their calculations. The last two things you can do is figure the volume of this mass of paper. This shows how much space is taken up needlessly in your local landfill. Find the turn-in cost of a pound of paper in your area. Multiply this by the final poundage number. You will be amazed at the amount of money that can be generated from a little conservation effort.
5. The book exercise fortunately/unfortunately is an excellent take-off book for this next idea. Write fortunately and unfortunately panels focusing on water, air and other environmental pollutants. Show what is unfortunate about each item illustrated in the first panel. Then in the second panel show how it can, fortunately, be prevented or corrected.
6. Make valentines in your class that can be sent to people that are environmentally doing good jobs. Pick the class' best ten poems for an environmental newspaper.

   Roses are red.
   Violets are blue.
   Thanks for helping our environment.
   From the kids in room 202 (two O two).
7. Discuss what universal signs are with your students. Show them some of the symbols that are used throughout the world. Then have them design universal symbols that would remind people to take care of our environment. Environmental symbols for clean streams, endangered species, pure air, acid rain, noise, hunting, car emissions and tree planting are some that can be developed.
8. Take a trip to your local water purification facility.
9. Your local garbage disposal company will gladly send someone to talk about recycling.

Write Like a Master

Complete the story starters below using the theme that some major/minor pollution or littering problem is growing out of proportion. It is starting to be a hazard and great annoyance. You need help. However, you feel your friends don't have the same concern for the environment as you do.

Story Starter I

That water is so thick with pollutants that you could walk across it and not get wet. The river looks like Jell-O. It is a disgrace! What would cause a town to allow this to get out of control? Someone, surely, has his eyes closed. What is going on around here? Look at that stuff oozing out of that factory's pipes. It's____

Story Starter II

It is my favorite television show. I just love it when the announcer says, "And now another true story from the pages of Enviroman's life. Remember, Enviroman protects our present and our future against the forces of evil and uncaring." I shiver to think how unlivable our world would be without him. Just think back to two years ago when____________________________

Story Starter III

You are holding the world's last flower, and it is as if no one cares. The flower is our last glimpse of nature's beauty and a shocking reminder of the stupidity of man. It needs our help. It needs to be ____

Story Starter IV

Buy Nopollute the greatest liquid since milk. All your environmental problems will be solved in each drop of its tiny space. Connect it to your garden hose and just ____________________

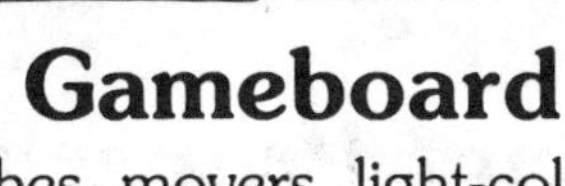

Gameboard

Materials Needed: Two number cubes, movers, light-colored crayons; Vexing Vocabulary; Just the Facts; student-made and teacher-made question cards can be placed in the areas provided for them in the center of the gameboard. They are optional but highly recommended. A card is picked each time a player has a multiple of five points in his/her bank (5, 10, 15, 20 or 25).

Players Needed: Two to four players or teams of two players

Play Procedures: Players alternate turns; throw number cubes; move in either direction at any time. This allows for playing strategies, rather than just mindlessly moving around a gameboard.

The Roll: Roll both number cubes. Your teacher will tell you to conduct some math operations with the number cubes. The three rules used most often in my classroom are

(a) Subtract the smaller from the larger; then move that many spaces (6 - 4 = <u>2</u>). Move two spaces.

(b) Multiply the two cubes and move the number of spaces in the one's column of the answer (2 x 6 = 1<u>2</u>). Move two spaces.

(c) Keep on adding the two cubes until you get one digit as the answer (6 + 6 = 12, 12 = 1 + 2 = 3). Move three spaces. Mathematicians call this finding the digital root.

Object: To score twenty-five points or to capture four pollution problems, future ideas and resorts. Owning a resort, pollutant or futuristic idea can be accomplished by landing on them in a normal turn, trading for them when you land on a trading post or buying one of them for two times their value when you land on the bank. Children like making the properties on scraps of paper before the game begins for easier exchange and banking. Each time you land on a property you color in (or initial) the little block in the corner of the property and put the points in your running bank. Ownership will change after trades only. Cross them out on the score sheet and add them to the other column. A scoreboard is provided for you. Each time someone lands on your property, he must pay you the number of points indicated in the top right-hand corner. Each time you land on your own property, you receive twice the points shown.

Winning Sets: Pollutants (acid rain, oil spill, smog or plastics); resorts (Las Vegas, Disneyland, Sea World and Atlantic City); futurism (robots, flying cars, talking to appliances and intelligence nuts)

Player One's Properties/Score	Player Two's Properties/Score

Game Card Property Pieces

On this page are the twelve game pieces for *Just a Dream*. Cut them out and place them on oaktag to prolong their usability. Place a little box next to the gameboard as a storage area. Each time someone lands on an appropriate board space, he receives points and one of the game cards to verify property ownership. It also makes property trading much easier. The next time you play the game, design your own game card property pieces. Design a gameboard and create your own educational board game. Pick a theme. Then try to add important facts and intellectual flavor to your game.

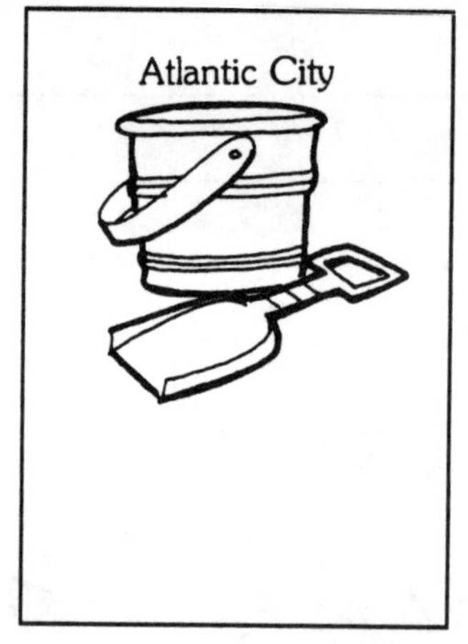

Future Dreams

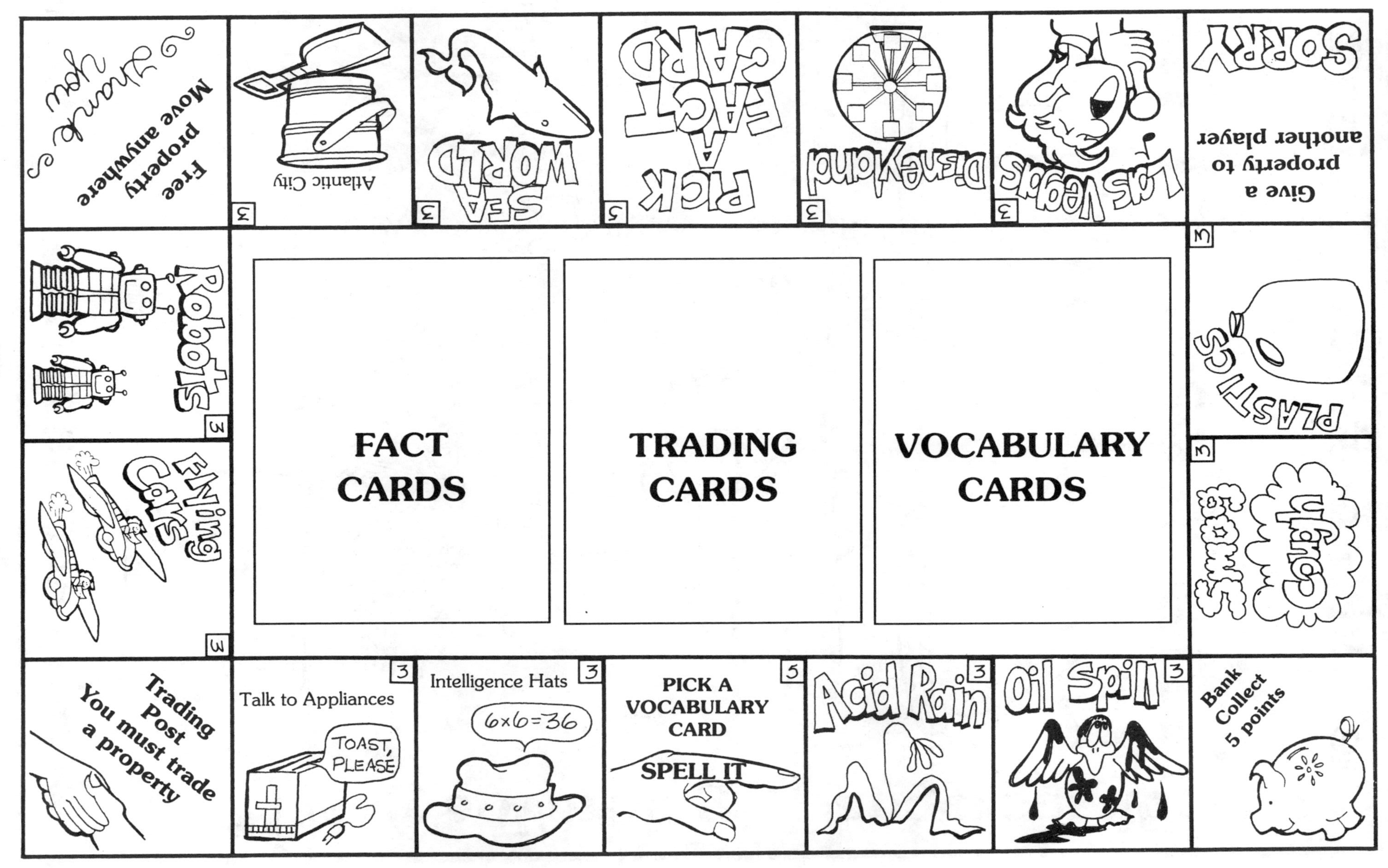

The Old Storyteller Flying Boats!

Charting a New Course An Ocean of Wonder

The Wreck of the Zephyr

This Way to the Flying Boats

Crash Landings Love of Sailing

The Master's Warning Dangerous Waters

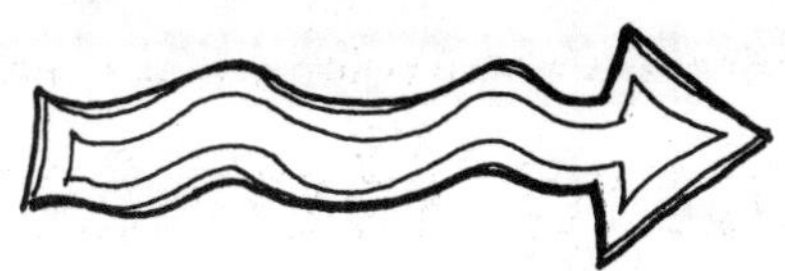

Lead-Ins to Literature

The Wreck of the Zephyr sounds like some kind of a disaster story involving a train or an airplane. A crash does play an important part in the story. However, the title seems to come from the theme of boats that can fly in the wind. Zephyr is the name of a certain type of wind in various parts of the world. It is also the story of a person striving to be the best he can be but taking shortcuts instead of learning the steps of the masters that attained the skill before him.

1. What other stories can you name that have a wreck/crash as an important part of the story?
____
____
2. In writing techniques, do you know what a flashback story is? Can you name two other stories that use the flashback technique? ____
____
3. What do you think a master of sailing might teach a new student? How do you think this might differ from teaching someone to drive? ____
____
4. Do you live in an area that is known for boating? ____
____
5. Are there any fishing experts in your area? ____
____
6. What water sports are available to people in your region? How far would you have to travel to the nearest pond, river, lake or ocean? ____
____
7. If you had the desire to be the greatest at something, would being a sailor be in your top five? Please explain why or why not. ____
____
8. Suppose you were easily susceptible to seasickness. Are there any jobs you could still do that would relate to the sailing industry in your town? ____
____
9. *Zephyr* seems to be a good name for a boat that will sail like the wind. What five names would be in your "boat name selection list"? ____
____
10. Sailors and books always seem to talk about the lure of the sea or ocean. What do you think lures people to the sea? Is that any different than what lures people to the mountains, forest or desert? ____
____
11. Can you name any famous sea captains who were trained by other famous sea captains? ____
____
____
12. Do you think the author/illustrator was influenced by the story of *Peter Pan* and its flying ship? ____
____
13. At what age should a person be allowed to sail solo on the ocean? ____

Just the Facts

1. What was the old man on the cliff overlooking the wrecked boat smoking? ______________

2. How did the old man say that the boat was carried that high up on the cliff? ______________

   ____

3. What is it hard to do over a flat sea? ______________________________

4. What kind of sky would warn the boy to stay in port? ______________________

5. Who is the only sailor that is capable of going out in terrible weather? ______________

6. *Blustery* is a word often used to describe ______________________________.

7. What part of the body did the boom strike? ______________________________

8. What was unique about the two boats that travelled past the cliff before he saw the boat that was towing the *Zephyr*? ______________________________

9. What does it mean when a boat is "beached"? ______________________________

10. His boat was so far from the water that the ______________________ couldn't even touch it.

11. What word was used to describe the reef that was around the mysterious new island? _____

    ____

12. The inhabitants on the new island almost never saw any ______________________ visit their shores or town.

13. Why couldn't the *Zephyr* fly? ______________________________

14. What kind of stew was served at dinner? ______________________________

15. ______________ ______________ tried to sail his ship over land and crashed.

16. A course for home was set by using the ______________________________.

17. What was the first thing that was spotted on the island that his village was on? ______________

18. The boat began to fall because of ______________________________.

19. After the boy crashed and grew up, how did he support himself? ______________________

20. What aided the storyteller as he limped back toward the harbor? ______________________

What Is Your Opinion?

1. We can sometimes feel when people are staring at us from behind. Do you think this is the same skill that would be involved in reading someone's mind? What do you know about mental telepathy? ______________________________

____

2. Who do you think are better storytellers, people who have lived the story, people who tell good made-up stories based somewhat on fact or those people who pass on the stories of their ancestors? Why? ______________________________

____

3. Would you have stayed to listen to this stranger's tale about the boat on the cliff? What do you think fascinates us the most about the tales old people tell? ______________________________

____

4. Sailing the seas as a master takes years of practice in many different types of unforseeable situations. Do you think that in a short time a boy could be a better sailor than the most experienced sailors in port? ______________________________

____

5. Would having a girl as the young sailor change the story in any way? How? ______________________________

____

____

6. The author doesn't use any names in the story. Does this add to the mystery of the people and places? ______________________________

____

7. The townspeople are hardly phased by seeing ships sailing in the air. Do you find this unusual? ______________________________

____

8. People always say, "It will take time to be good at...." What three things do they most often put in this category? Do you believe that it couldn't be done faster? Explain. ______________________________

____

____

9. Do you think the song about Samuel·Blue was the sailor's way of telling the boy not to be in a hurry, or was it just a song to follow a good meal? ______________________________

____

____

Vexing Vocabulary

breeze	flattest	*Zephyr*	Samuel
harbor	hoisted	blustery	churning
gust	cockpit	recognize	trimmed
bordered	unbelievable	pleaded	spire
treacherous	surrounded	reef	rustle
oyster	magically	concertina	remarkable

Can you write seven sentences incorporating the three vocabulary words going across each column in each of your sentences?

Example: The lack of a breeze didn't stop the *Zephyr* from sailing across the flattest part of the bay.

1. ______________________________
2. ______________________________
3. ______________________________
4. ______________________________
5. ______________________________
6. ______________________________
7. ______________________________

Pick five vocabulary words from the list above. Place them in alphabetical order. Then see if you can integrate them into a sentence in that same order.

Example: treacherous, Samuel, spire, surrounded, trimmed–Samuel, spire, surrounded, treacherous, trimmed. Samuel climbed the spire, pursued and surrounded by a treacherous mob barely trimmed by his excellent marksmanship.

Use the spaces below and create two alphabetical fives of your own. Follow the format in the example for each of your sentence creations.

1. ______________________________

2. ______________________________

Try the ultimate challenge of making every word in your sentence, including the five vocabulary words, in alphabetical order. Use the space below for your sentence.

____

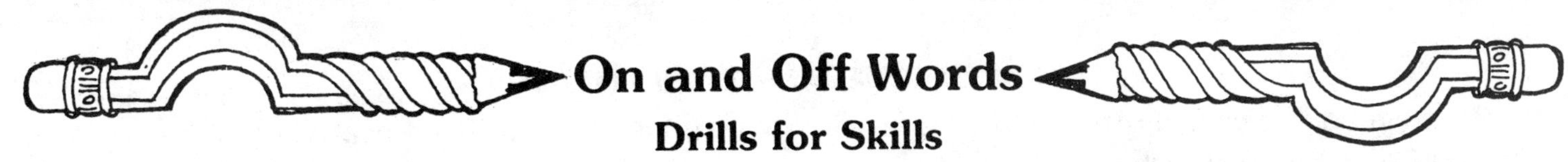

On and Off Words

Drills for Skills

Each clue below will generate a word that has *on* or *off* contained in it. After evaluating each clue and finding the correct answer, place the vowels in the answer over the total letters to find your score.

Clue	Answer	Fraction (V/TL)
Example: a drink	coffee	3/6 = 1/2
1. summer material	__________	________
2. burial box	__________	________
3. 2000 pounds	__________	________
4. not defense	__________	________
5. famous ape	__________	________
6. tip one's hat	__________	________
7. business place	__________	________
8. ________henge	__________	________
9. children	__________	________
10. ________ boom (speed)	__________	________
11. football penalty	__________	________
12. northwest state	__________	________
13. a kind of candy	__________	________
14. musical sound	__________	________
15. prairie schooner	__________	________
16. to insult	__________	________
17. to show scorn	__________	________
18. a contraction	__________	________

See how many additional words you can think of that contain *on* or *off* in them in exact order. Place your words in the two columns provided below.

ON	OFF
__________	__________
__________	__________
__________	__________
__________	__________

Ideas and Illustrations

You are taking your favorite sailboat to a sail judging contest on an island near your home. You will find four small sailboats below surrounding a larger sailboat. Place your four best designs on the smaller sailboats. Then choose your best sail drawing to be placed on the larger sailboat. Place your name on the keel of the larger boat. Take a piece of overhead transparency and trace maps showing the principal oceans or lakes of the world. Blow these transparencies up to mural size and place your boat and your classmates' boats in settings on the map. Your boats might be used to trace famous sea routes in history. You might want to just take a leisurely sail on the Great Lakes, to Catalina or Mystic Island. My imaginary sailboat would be placed on Singer Island off the coast of Florida. My sister chose any water near Hawaii. Anyone for the Bering Sea next to Alaska?

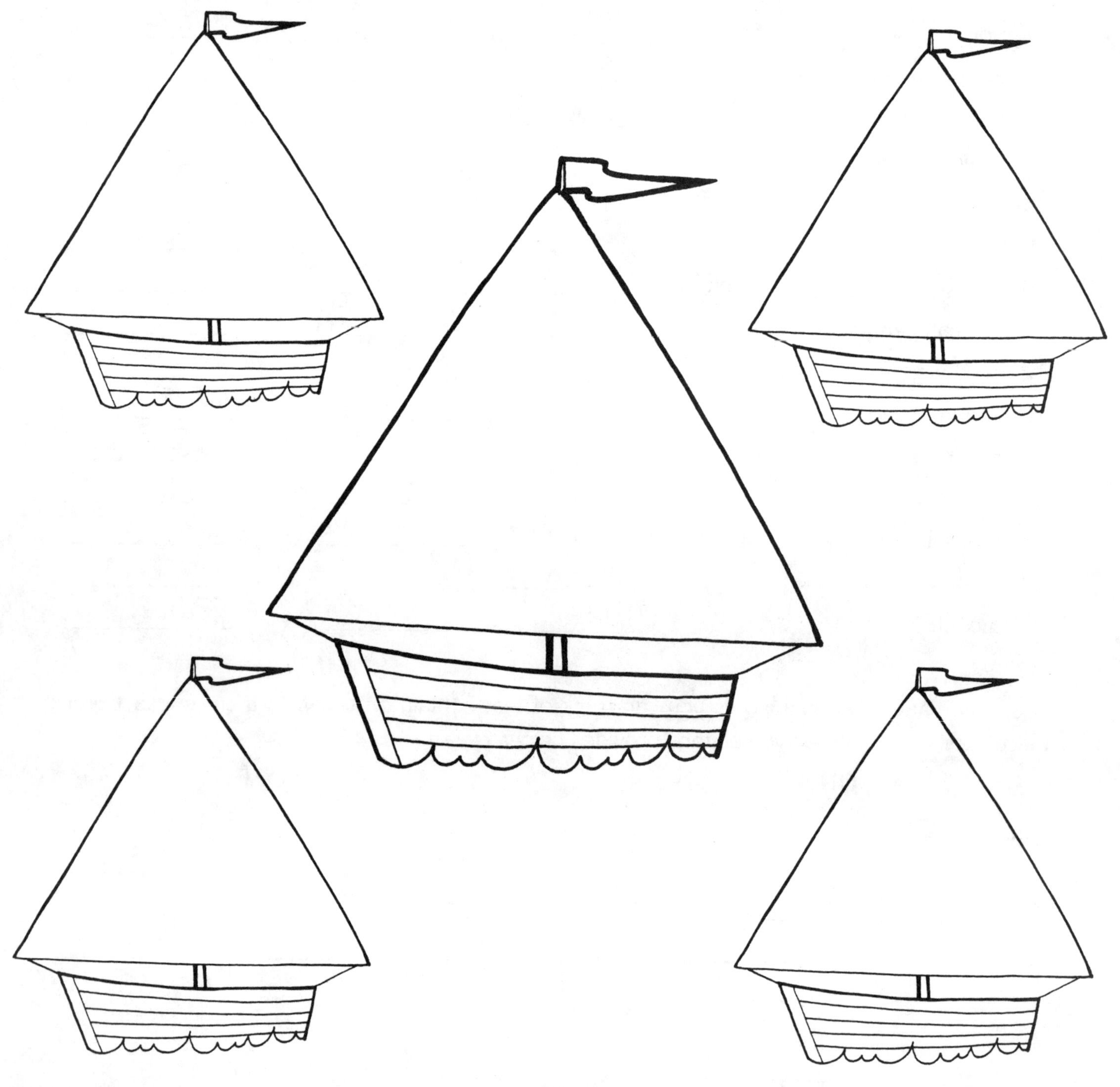

Short-Term Project

There is a tremendous amount of creativity in the naming of one's boat. Hang around any dock and you will see names of nautical significance (*Trafalgar*) to family fun (*All Smiths*). My two favorites *Naughty Naughty* with a rowboat on its deck, *Just a Little Bit Naughty* and *Bermuda Schwartz* led me to think up a classroom activity for creatively naming boats. The rules are simple. You must use a nautical or boating term in your title. The name has to be appropriate for a certain occupation or particular person. I had so much fun making up names that I think I exhausted every possible idea that could be used. After reading the list below and discussing the significance of each title with your classmates, see if you can create five names for boats that might have been overlooked.

	Owner's Name or Job	Vessel's Name
1.	nurse	I Sea U
2.	teacher	Astern
3.	restaurant owner	Crab Cakes
4.	gangster	Get My Drift
5.	rap rock group	Fat Homs
6.	storekeeper	Sale Boat
7.	choir director	Coral Group
8.	fish store owner	Scale Ups (Scallops)
9.	Lee Trevino	Fore Birdie
10.	weight lifter	Reel Man
11.	Reggie Jackson	Big Leagues
12.	Tony Perkins	Baits Motel
13.	Santa Claus	Christmas Reef
14.	jockey	Shore Thing
15.	baker	O Lee O
16.	carpenter	Sandy Craft
17.	newscaster	Channel 5
18.	preacher	Thou Shell Not
19.	doctor	Buoy Your Spirits
20.	TV repairman	Tuna Station
21.	electrician	That's Sharking
22.	comedienne	D Aft
23.	art teacher	Drawbridge
24.	gambler	D Eel
25.	miner	Sunken Treasure
26.	photographer	Galley Proof
27.	aerobics instructor	Shipshape

Place your five selections on the blanks below.

1. ______________________________
2. ______________________________
3. ______________________________
4. ______________________________
5. ______________________________

Famous Ships of Fact and Fiction

Research Suggestions I

Famous Ships of Fact and Fiction focuses on those ships that have distinguished themselves in the annals of history or literature. You are to research two ships in the historical area and two ships in the area of literature. Your information should contain your sources, illustrations, graphs and charts.

Some suggested topics might involve research about the

Argos	*Mayflower*	*Queen Elizabeth*
Half Moon	*Niña, Pinta* and *Santa María*	*Robert E. Lee*
United States	*Jolly Roger*	*Bismarck*
Mimi	*Nautilus*	*Savanna*
Old Ironsides	*Monitor, Merrimac*	*Clermont*
Trieste	*Titanic*	*Victoria*

The four ships I am researching are

1. ______________________________
2. ______________________________
3. ______________________________
4. ______________________________

My sources of information were

1. ______________________________
2. ______________________________
3. ______________________________
4. ______________________________

I spoke to the following experts/people about my research:

1. ______________________________
2. ______________________________
3. ______________________________
4. ______________________________

I discovered these three additional facts about ships:

1. ______________________________
2. ______________________________
3. ______________________________

Ships of Fact and Fiction

Research Suggestions II

The paper below has been divided into two sections with two boxes in each section. The left-hand boxes should highlight your two fictional ships, while the right-hand section will house your two ships of fact. Make your drawings as close to the originals as possible. Please do not copy their pictures and put them in these positions. After using this page for planning and teacher and peer input, create a mini mural on 11" x 14" (27.94 x 35.56 cm) paper with drawings of all four vessels. Come up with a unique title for your mural such as "The Great Sailing Ships."

Fictional Ship	**Actual Model**

Fictional Ship	**Actual Ship**

Teacher Suggestions

The world of the sea and the ships that have travelled the sea from the Norsemen to Phoenicians to nuclear submariners is filled with exciting research topics. We Philadelphians are lucky to have one of the finest maritime museums in the country at our fingertips. If your fingertips can touch only the encyclopedia at your local library, the older the encyclopedia, the better the information on early ships.

1. Research the sea drawings of Winslow Homer (1836-1910) and compare his drawings to those of Chris Van Allsburg in *The Wreck of the Zephyr*. What other artists are known for their depictions of the sea, and how do they compare to Van Allsburg's drawings? My favorite is the river drawings of Thomas Eakins (1844-1916).
2. Discuss the exploits of Magellan and his fleet. Juan Sebastian Del Cano on September 6, 1522, was the first to sail around the world in Magellan's ship, *Victoria*. Why then is Magellan always given this honor?
3. Create a ship time line with your class. Place a drawing of each ship in question, as well as what it was famous for above the date on the time line. Examples of important dates might be 3500 B.C. (first sail invented); 1492 A.D. (Columbus discovers America); 1522 A.D. (*Victoria* sails around the world); 1807 (*Clermont,* first steam-powered passenger ship), etc. Try to add little known ships to your chart in addition to the more famous ones.
4. Have an Our Ship Is in Port Day. Divide the class into crews. Each crew will have to select and represent a certain ship time period–Norsemen, Egyptians, Minoan/Mycenaean, Phoenician, Roman, Italian, English, clipper, steamboat, propeller driven, nuclear powered. They then make a drawing or model of their ship and dress as the crew or passengers would dress. Songs of the sea could be researched from each period. Foods matching the nautical decor could be served. Most classes have Salute the Country Day. This would have the same format.
5. "I Would Like to Be Taught by These Famous Ship Captains" is an excellent research topic for students to explore. Please have each student tell why he would like to be taught by Lord Nelson, Francis Drake, Henry Hudson, Lewis and Clark and others. He should, also, indicate the exact knowledge that will be learned.
6. Bring a *Who's Who* book into class and devise "Who's Who" lists for boating, books, movies, TV and history. Follow this with cutouts and stories. Show the five best dressed and worst dressed stars or book characters. The children should build a portfolio of their choices.
7. Very little can be found about famous shipwrecks. Hopefully, a little used book appears in your local library.
8. Ask your students to design seaworthy ship models. Launch them down a ramp of poured water into a metal washtub in a classroom boat christening ceremony. Points are recorded for best design, sea worthiness and launch.
9. Design three sails for a wind surfer's rigging.

Write Like a Master

The theme for these story starters is the beauty, danger and mystery of the ocean. The variety of writing situations will allow you to try to make some of your points serious and some humorous. In either case, try to make your points somewhat believable. Please don't re-create the Lock Ness Monster. Instead, try to write what actually might have happened or what would have been said in such a situation.

Story Starter I

We are taking on water! One more big wave and we will capsize. Keep pumping and bailing with those buckets. I'm not sure my S.O.S. got out before the radio went dead. This storm has pushed us miles off the course where most rescuers would expect us to be. Try to ____________

____

____

____

____

Story Starter II

Good old Uncle George, "the world's greatest giftgiver"! What is an eleven-year-old boy going to do with a sailboat when the nearest lake, river or pond is over four hundred miles away? Uncle George wasn't joking when he sent it to me, and it looks quite expensive, so maybe this is some kind of test. Maybe he wants to see if I'll ____________________

____

____

____

____

Story Starter III

Welcome to Oceanic World, Walt Disney's newest theme park. Enjoy the world's greatest and most challenging waters brought to you in the world's newest technology, "aquaholography." Everything you touch is real and everything that touches you is ____________________

____

____

____

____

Story Starter IV

Look, I told you, the wedding is off. They're my family and no one is going to make fun of them. No, it is not marry me, marry my family. It's just a matter of respect. ____________________

____

____

____

____

Gameboard

Materials Needed: Two number cubes, movers, light-colored crayons; Vexing Vocabulary; Just the Facts; student-made and teacher-made question cards can be placed in the areas provided for them in the center of the gameboard. They are optional but highly recommended. A card is picked each time a player has a multiple of five points in his/her bank (5, 10, 15, 20 or 25).

Players Needed: Two to four players or teams of two players

Play Procedures: Players alternate turns; throw number cubes; move in either direction at any time. This allows for playing strategies, rather than just mindlessly moving around a gameboard.

The Roll: Roll both number cubes. Your teacher will tell you to conduct some math operations with the number cubes. The three rules used most often in my classroom are

(a) Subtract the smaller from the larger; then move that many spaces (6 - 4 = 2). Move two spaces.

(b) Multiply the two cubes and move the number of spaces in the one's column of the answer (2 x 6 = 12). Move two spaces.

(c) Keep on adding the two cubes until you get one digit as the answer (6 + 6 = 12, 12 = 1 + 2 = 3). Move three spaces. Mathematicians call this finding the digital root.

Object: To score twenty-five points or to capture four ships, islands or bodies of water. Owning ships, islands and bodies of water can be accomplished by landing on them in a normal turn, trading for them when you land on a trading post or buying one of them for two times their value when you land on the bank. Each time you land on a property you color in (or initial) the little block in the corner of the property and put the points in your running bank. Ownership will change after trades only. Cross them out on the score sheet and add them to the other column. A scoreboard is provided for you. Each time someone lands on your property, he must pay you the number of points indicated in the top right-hand corner. Each time you land on your own property, you receive twice the points shown.

Winning Sets: Ships (*Titanic, Nautilus, Argos* and *Half Moon*); islands (Australia, Catalina, Hawaii and Manhattan); water bodies (Bering Sea, Lake Superior, Arctic Ocean and English Channel)

Player One's Properties/Score	Player Two's Properties/Score

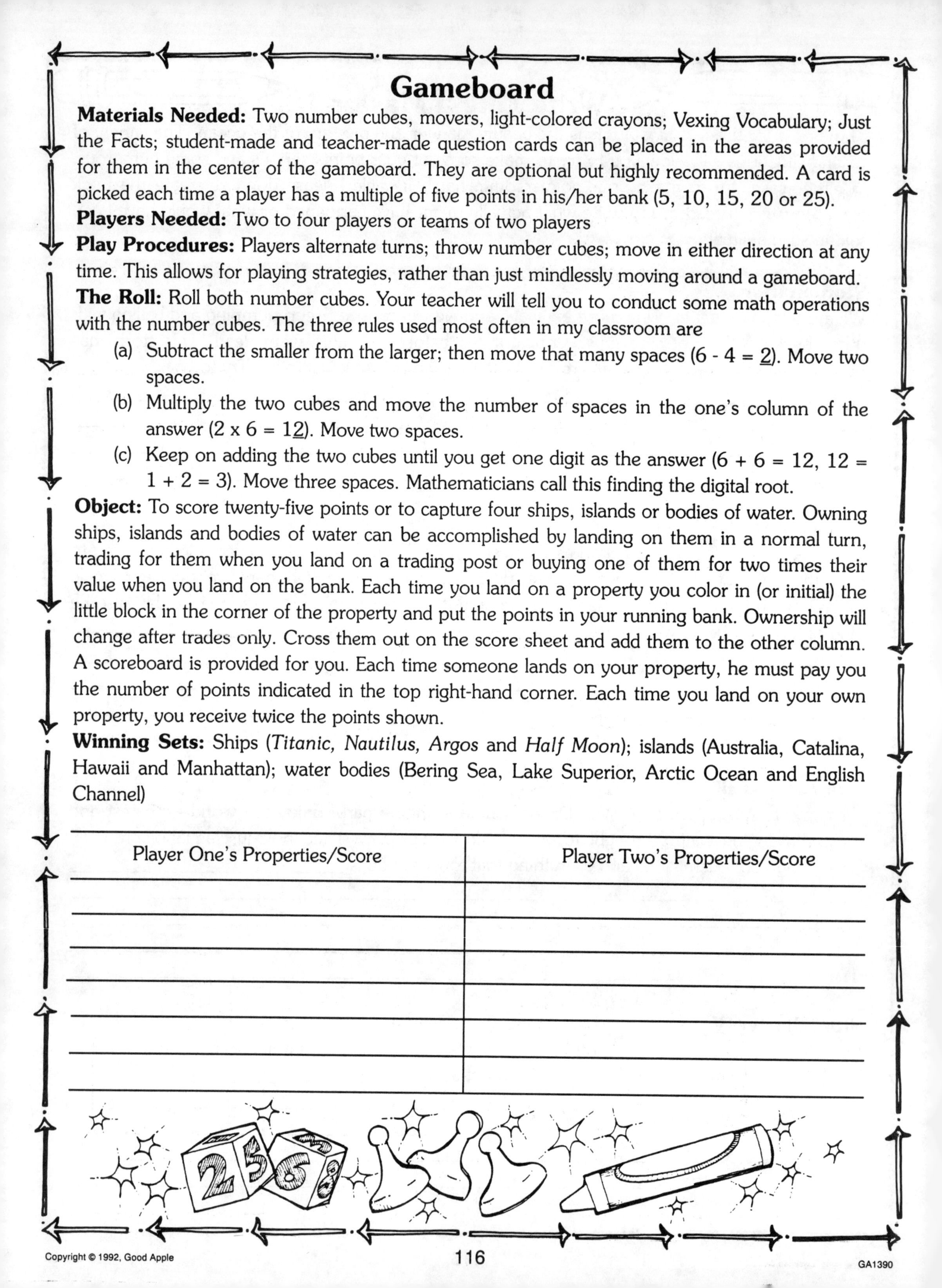

Game Card Property Pieces

On this page are the twelve game pieces for *The Wreck of the Zephyr*. Cut them out and place them on oaktag to prolong their usability. Place a little box next to the gameboard as a storage area. Each time someone lands on an appropriate board space, he receives points and one of the game cards to verify property ownership. It also makes property trading much easier. The next time you play the game, design your own game card property pieces. Deisgn a gameboard and create your own educational board game. Pick a theme. Then try to add important facts and intellectual flavor to your game.

From Ship to Shore

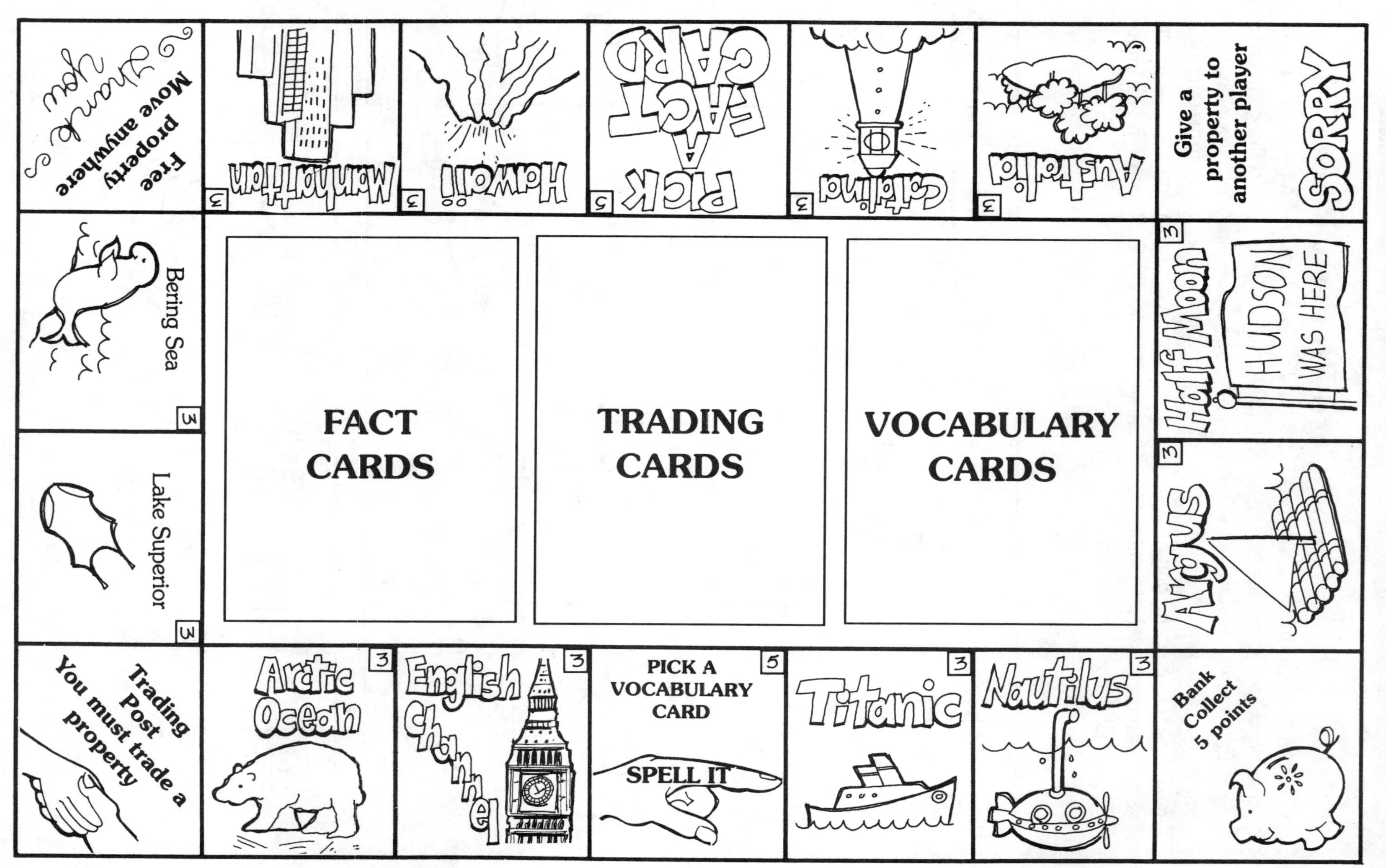

The Great Sphinx | A Great Flood

Ben's Dream

Sleepy Studying

Floating Houses

China's Great Wall

The Eiffel Tower

Shared Dreams | Geography Test

Lead-Ins to Literature

I hope you are not the type of person that gets seasick easily. *Ben's Dream* is going to take you by boat, I mean house, to see the landmarks of the world. Some people will do anything to get out of a test. Ben decides to get out of his geography test by sailing his house around the world. Is it just a dream or has Ben discovered the adventure of a lifetime? Read *Ben's Dream* and decide for yourself. If this book can get you out of taking a test, it must certainly be worth reading.

1. If you could get out of one test this year, in what subject area would that test be? Why?
2. Ben is going to visit some of the world's famous landmarks. Predict three places that you think he would visit.
3. Bike riding is woven, in a minor way, into the story. What ways would you use a bike in a typical children's story? What new, never-thought-of ideas for a bike can you devise?
4. If you could go on a boat cruise, what place would you like to see? Please explain why and give some information about your trip. Are there special sites involved in your voyage?
5. Why do you think people like to read stories that talk about dreams?
6. Has anyone ever told you about his dreams? If so, what were the key points of his dreams?
7. Who would you take with you in a dream?
8. Everything in *Ben's Dream* is covered in water. Why do you think the author used water this way?
9. Ben and his friend Margaret are running away from a rainstorm. What three things would you tell a person to do, and not to do, if he were caught in a thunderstorm?
10. In your area could water play an important role in a story? How would the water around you be used in a story? Why would water adventures interest you if you did not have any water in your area?
11. Do you think it is possible that two or more people could have the same exact dream?
12. If you were going to sail your house around the world, what special features would you add to the house to make it seaworthy? What type of items would you take with you to insure your safety and unquenchable appetite for all foods?

Just the Facts

1. When Ben returned home from his bike ride, Ben's mother was not home. Where was she?

 ____

2. What type of rain clouds chased Ben and Margaret home from their planned afternoon of play? ____

 ____

3. What activity did Ben and Margaret have to postpone because of the rain? ____________

4. When was the geography test? ______________________________

5. What held Mom's note to the kitchen cabinet? ______________________

6. Where did Ben do his studying? ______________________________

7. What kind of sound did the rain make? ______________________

8. What awoke Ben in his dream? ______________________________

9. The first landmark in his dream was the ______________________.

10. When the house passed Big Ben, what time did the clock hands show? ____________

11. The Leaning Tower of Pisa seems to be bobbing in the water the same way a channel ____ does.

12. What was around the Great Sphinx? ______________________

13. Who yelled for Ben to wake up? ______________________

14. After Ben was awakened by Margaret, what did he take outside with him? ____________

 Why? ____

15. In the dream Margaret and Ben met/waved to each other at the ______________.

 They were both on their ______________________________.

16. What portion of each landmark was under water? ______________________

17. Ben and Margaret walked their bikes over what area near Ben's house? ____________

18. What was the last landmark in *Ben's Dream*? ______________________

19. Who are the four faces on Mount Rushmore? ______________________

20. What put Ben and Margaret to sleep? ______________________

21. What did Margaret drop in amazement? ______________________

What Is Your Opinion?

1. If you were riding your bike and storm clouds were quickly approaching, would you race for home or find the nearest safe shelter? Please explain.________________________

   ____

2. Give a funny answer for which you think is more important, studying for a geography test or playing baseball? ____________________________________

3. What is your ideal place to study for a test? Tell it in a manner that would encourage others to change their ideal studying places to yours? ________________________

   ____

4. Of the landmarks presented in the book, which do you think is the greatest one? Why? Can you think of three other landmarks that should be included in a list of greatest landmarks?___

   ____

5. Rain tends to put many people to sleep. Can you name five things that you think are great sleep helpers?____

   ____

6. If you were a doctor and one of your patients kept dreaming of famous landmarks, what two things would you prescribe to stop this from happening? Why do you think your patient is dreaming of landmarks? ____________________________________

   ____

7. Water appears in many dreams. Why do you think this happens so often? __________

   ____

8. What is so unusual about two people having the same exact dream? Why do you think they waved to each other in the dream?________________________________

   ____

9. Do you think there was something magical about Ben and Margaret's geography book? Please explain. ____

   ____

10. Many authors develop porches into their stories. What is so special about having a front porch? If most people don't have a porch, how can they relate to a porch in a story?______

    ____

11. A dropped jaw indicates surprise. Name three other gestures that an author might use. Explain what they mean. ____________________________________

    ____

12. What is the most enjoyable thing about bike riding? The least enjoyable? __________

    ____

13. What would Ben dream about if he had a literature test? __________________

    ____

Creative Configuration Wordcrosses

Vexing Vocabulary

geography	Margaret	pedaled	statue
landmark	easy chair	downpour	Eiffel
sphinx	amazement	rhythmic	Pisa
drumming	porch	gravel	leaning
sleepyhead	jaw	gosh	mosque
mitt	rough	world	Rushmore

In *Integrating the Literature of Beverly Cleary in the Classroom*, synonym wordcrosses were discussed. It involved crossing a word with its synonym at a letter both words had in common. For instance, the word *statue* would be crossed by the word *figure* at the letter *U*.

```
    F
    I
    G
STATUE
    R
    E
```

Configuration wordcrosses need not be synonyms. They may exhibit creative word ideas and designs which will help your mind to recall these same words and their surrounding ideas at a later date. See how many creative combinations for the twenty-four vocabulary words you can form. Some are completed for you. You may have another way these words can also be combined.

```
  R              T                                 P       S
MOUNT            O        EASY CHAIR            BIKE     EGYPT
  S              W                 E               D       H
  H           EIFFEL               L               A       I
  M              R                 A               L       N
  O                                X               E       X
  R                                                D
  E
```

PORCH MARGARET GRAVEL

MITT DRUMMING RHYTHMIC DOWNPOUR

See if you can fit all twenty-four words and their partners on this page. Transfer your ideas to larger paper. Writing the words with colored pencils brightens up your work. Place illustrations next to each combination to bring further attention to your work. Pick ten historic sites and complete their wordcrosses and illustrations. Try doing this for cities throughout the world. Cross Paris with Eiffel Tower, New York with Empire State Building, London with Big Ben, St. Louis with Gateway Arch, your town with....

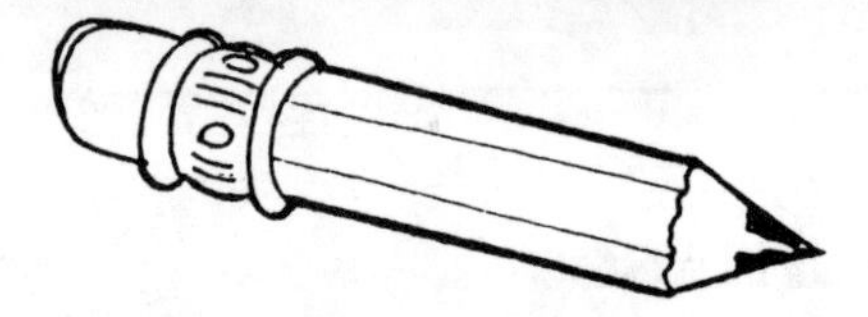
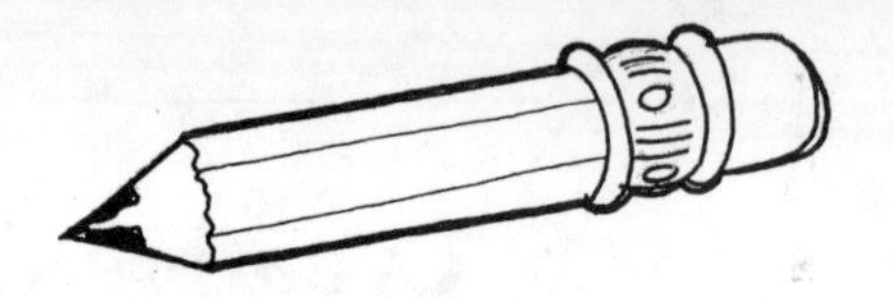

Drills for Skills

It is strange that only two names, Ben and Margaret, are used in the story. Maybe Chris Van Allsburg should have completed the following activity in school. He would then have had more children's names at the tip of his pen. You will find common and not so common name endings below. See if you can find names that end with each ending. The first one in each group is completed for you. Please complete the remaining four. Form a group of five students to compare answers. Score one point for each name you have on your list that is not on anyone else's list.

Word ending ___ IS
1. JANIS
2. ____________
3. ____________
4. ____________
5. ____________

Word ending ___ ERT
1. ROBERT
2. ____________
3. ____________
4. ____________
5. ____________

Word ending ___ AS
1. THOMAS
2. ____________
3. ____________
4. ____________
5. ____________

Word ending ___ DA
1. YOLANDA
2. ____________
3. ____________
4. ____________
5. ____________

Word ending ___ IN
1. ROBIN
2. ____________
3. ____________
4. ____________
5. ____________

Word ending ___ MY
1. TAMMY
2. ____________
3. ____________
4. ____________
5. ____________

Word ending ___ EN
1. CARMEN
2. ____________
3. ____________
4. ____________
5. ____________

Word ending ___ IL
1. NEIL
2. ____________
3. ____________
4. ____________
5. ____________

Word ending ___ OR
1. ELEANOR
2. ____________
3. ____________
4. ____________
5. ____________

On the back of this page develop five name endings of your own. Get a classmate to help you form your lists. What ending would you predict ends the most names? At least two letters must appear in your ending.

Baseball and Landmark Cards

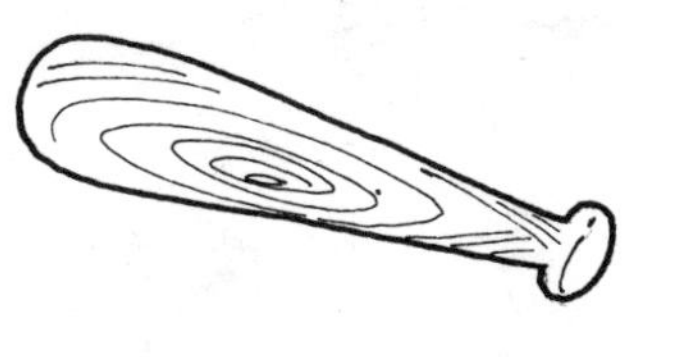

Ideas and Illustrations

The outlines of four different types of baseball cards have been provided for you below. Before designing these four cards with your own individual ideas, examine the card designs of the major companies (Fleer, Donruss, Topps, Upper Deck, Sportflic, Classic and Leaf). Look at the companies 3-D effects, holograms, artwork, statistical charts and special photography techniques before designing/starting your creations. Put your pictures, your classmates, movie and music stars on your work. Other variations could include cards depicting the landmarks of the world, great books, famous scientists, minority contributors, monsters, myths or famous women. Try designing a card to represent each Chris Van Allsburg book featured in this book.

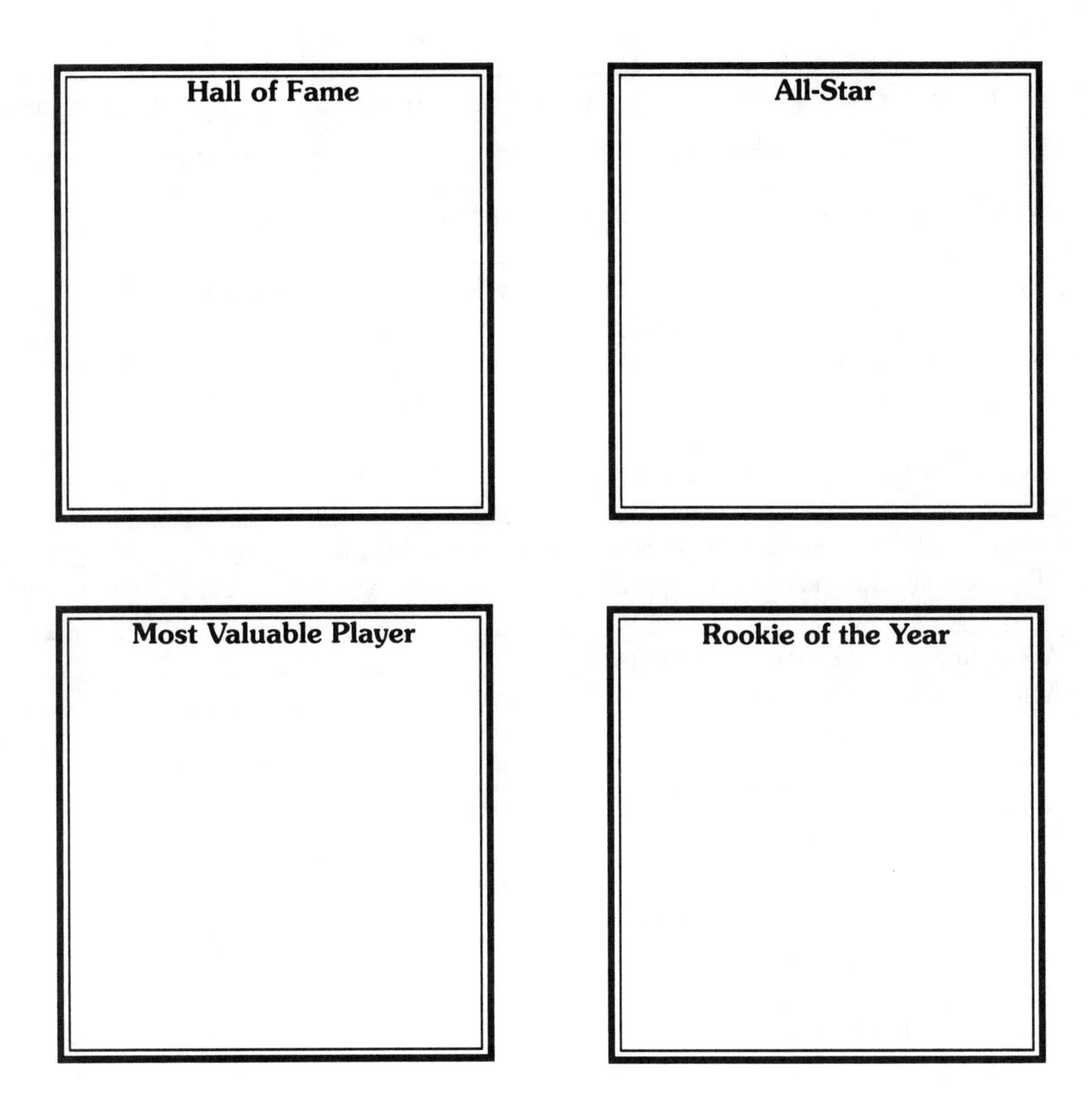

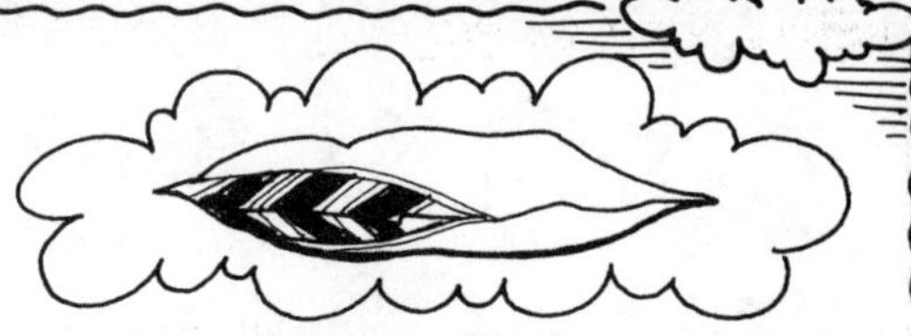

Dream Survey

Short-Term Project

Imagine that you live in an age where you can program your own dreams before going to bed each night. This is accomplished by feeding the form below through a special spot on your pillow. Please complete this form. Put it under your pillow tonight. Report to your classmates the things that appeared on your form that also appeared in your dream. Yes, it is weird, but try it anyway!

1. What type of dream would you like to have? Please explain so we are able to form your dream exactly the way you want it to happen. Tonight's choices include everyday life, historical setting, underwater exploration, sports event, medical or child-care profession, mystery, dream vacation. Other ____________________
   Dream type requested ____________________
   Reason ____________________
   ____
2. If you have an exact location for your dream, please record it. If you do not, the computer will pick one for you. ____________________
   ____
3. What family members and friends would you like to have participate? __________
   ____
4. What people outside your friends and family would you like to have participate? __________
   ____
5. Your favorite color will be used throughout the scenery. What is your favorite color, and how much would you like to see it used? Large, medium or small amount? __________
   ____
6. Would you like your dream to have a happy, sad or to-be-continued ending like a mini series? Please explain. ____________________
7. What animals/insects shouldn't appear in your nightly dream? __________
8. What animals should appear in your dream, and what name would you like to give to each?
   ____
9. What time in history would you like to visit? Why? ____________________
10. Where would you like a vacation dream to take you? ____________________
11. What all-purpose items would you like to take with you in the dream? __________
12. What money amount under $1000 dollars would you like to have supplied? __________
13. Would you like your age to be changed in the dream? ____________________
    What age would you like? Why? ____________________
14. Would you like a printout before your dream takes place so you can make corrections or after your dream so you can be surprised? Please explain. ____________________
    ____

Describe tonight's dream on the back of this sheet in your own words so the computer can check its settings. Draw a scene from the dream so the computer can check its tints and colors.

Research Suggestions

1. At what world landmark would you like to work as a tour guide? Write a tour guide speech describing the landmark to a group of tourists. Try to find some facts that few people know about the landmark. This can be done with a local museum or three pictures from an art book. Sports lovers can do this for a stadium like the Houston or New Orleans Astro/Super Domes.

2. Have you ever seen a limited edition plate? Draw five large circles on a piece of drawing paper. Use landmarks as a theme to design five limited edition plates. If you aren't a great artist, use cutouts to assist your design work.

3. Create a Landmarks of the World board game. Make a set of twenty question cards that can be used when players land on a "Do you know these landmark facts" box.

4. Research bike races that are held in your area. What are some of the rules that everyone should know about bike racing?

5. Draw two bike racing courses, one using the streets and roads in your area and one using a large stadium.

6. Design a new Mount Rushmore using the faces of present day political heroes, sports stars, movie stars, scientists or musicians.

7. Write one inning of a baseball game broadcast focusing on each team's strengths and weaknesses. Draw a picture of the broadcast booth, stadium or a scene from the game. See if you can arrange for a class visit to a local radio station or for two or three members of your class to attend a baseball game in the announcer's booth.

8. Design a survey that will ask your classmates questions about their dreams.

9. Do a mini paper on the geography of the area in which you live.

10. Write a mini story about "the worst rainstorm ever and I'm not kidding."

11. Design a furniture catalog featuring "the best easy chairs of today, tomorrow and yesterday."

12. Have you ever been to a home show? Pick five common kitchen features. Show or describe how they might change in the future. Do this for other items around your house.

13. Research how a rain gauge works, and draw a rain map of your state. What three United States areas get the most rain? Least?

Tour Guide

Teacher Suggestions

1. Make a "How Can We Get There" chart featuring your hometown and the distances to each of the landmarks in *Ben's Dream.* Research three airlines, their flight schedules and landmark visitation costs. Write the Holiday Inn or Marriot Corporation for rates and nearest hotels to each landmark.
2. Give each of your students a T-shirt outline. Each is to design a T-shirt that would be sold in front of each landmark in *Ben's Dream*. Have students transfer their ideas on actual T-shirts. Most computers have a T-shirt transfer program on which T-shirts can also be designed. Your computer lab teacher knows about the special ribbon that is necessary to accomplish this task.
3. Have a local bicycle shop owner come to your class to talk about new bicycle designs, their repairs and safeguards.
4. After discussing landmarks, have your class create a landmark that would attract people to your hometown.
5. Design a classroom mural titled "The History of Timepieces and Famous Clocks of the World." Have each child research a timepiece (hourglass, sundial, water clock, cuckoo clock, etc.). Mount each child's drawings and information on a giant piece of butcher paper for display.
6. Discuss with your class their favorite computer games and the aspects of each game that make them so challenging, enjoyable and stimulating. Discuss how teaching about landmarks can be incorporated into a computer game.
7. Research the Statue of Liberty's history and recent restoration. Write for information about how a site becomes a national landmark. Local buildings can be considered national landmarks. Find out about your state's procedures for declaring a local site a landmark.
8. Pick five landmarks, national parks or museums that members of your class have visited. Make an age graph showing the approximate age of each child when he visited the site. Disneyland and Disney World; the Cooperstown Hall of Fame; the Liberty Bell; MGM or Universal Studio's Theme Park; Old Faithful; Mount Rushmore; Statue of Liberty; Niagara Falls; The Alamo; Valley Forge; the homes of Lincoln, Washington and Edison could be included.
9. Research five other books where water is an important part of the theme. The Wicked Witch of the West, William Tell, "The Ugly Duckling" and *The Witch of Blackbird Pond* make good discussion topics. Age levels will vary.
10. Investigate sleep research with your class. Pick a simple sleep research theme that can be conducted by your students. Pick an exact time that everyone can go to sleep. Each student records the hour that he wakes up, even if it is in the middle of the night. What kind of sleep predictions can be made from the class findings?
11. Design an historic site food menu or a fast food that can be sold nationwide such as Big Ben Burgers, a pitcher of Hall of Fame soda.
12. Of the landmarks in *Ben's Dream*, the Taj Mahal is the one we know the least about. Have an A to Z scavenger hunt finding facts about the Taj Mahal.

Write Like a Master

The theme for these story starters will focus on our national or world historical monuments. Try to weave a famous location into each story starter below. Make the reader think that he is really there. Use creative descriptive techniques as you describe each landmark in your stories. Place an illustration next to each story starter.

Story Starter I

I'm slipping! If someone doesn't grab hold of me soon, tomorrow's paper is going to carry the story of the first eleven-year-old to fall off the Eiffel Tower. Why did I take the dare of walking on the protective guardrail? This guide wire that stopped my fall is the only thing between me, the pavement and a front page headline. I can't tell if anyone even sees me here. The wire is cutting into my gloves and ______________________________

____

____

____

Story Starter II

If the Great Sphinx, the mighty guardian of the desert and secret keeper of the pharaohs, could talk, its favorite tale would have school children all over America amazed when it starts to talk about______________________________

____

____

Story Starter III

The Great Wall of China Bike Race is every school child's dream. Since my first training wheels, I imagined racing against the best bicyclists in the world at any age level, of course I often made up races and announced them to myself as I was riding on my bike. Now I am really here, thanks to______________________________

____

____

Story Starter IV

My dad designed Mount Rushmore and chiseled away at the figures for years. He ______________

____

____

____

Story Starter V

If they asked me, I could straighten out the Leaning Tower of Pisa in no time. First, I'd__________

____

____

____

Gameboard

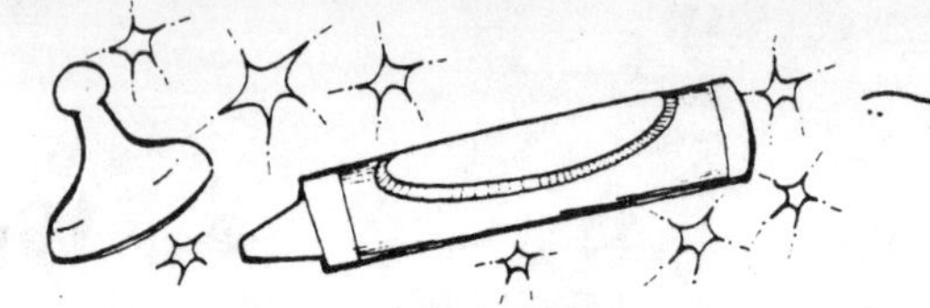

Materials Needed: Two number cubes, movers, light-colored crayons; Vexing Vocabulary; Just the Facts; student-made and teacher-made question cards can be placed in the areas provided for them in the center of the gameboard. They are optional but highly recommended. A card is picked each time a player has a multiple of five points in his/her bank (5, 10, 15, 20 or 25).

Players Needed: Two to four players or teams of two players

Play Procedures: Players alternate turns; throw number cubes; move in either direction at any time. This allows for playing strategies, rather than just mindlessly moving around a gameboard.

The Roll: Roll both number cubes. Your teacher will tell you to conduct some math operations with the number cubes. The three rules used most often in my classroom are

(a) Subtract the smaller from the larger; then move that many spaces (6 - 4 = 2). Move two spaces.

(b) Multiply the two cubes and move the number of spaces in the one's column of the answer (2 x 6 = 12). Move two spaces.

(c) Keep on adding the two cubes until you get one digit as the answer (6 + 6 = 12, 12 = 1 + 2 = 3). Move three spaces. Mathematicians call this finding the digital root.

Object: To score twenty-five points or to capture four structures, dreams and bedroom features and numbers. Owning a dream, world structure or bedroom furniture can be accomplished by landing on them in a normal turn, trading for them when you land on a trading post or buying one of them for two times their value when you land on the bank. Children like making the properties on scraps of paper before the game begins for easier exchange and banking. Each time you land on a property you color in (or initial) the little block in the corner of the property and put the points in your running bank. Ownership will change after trades only. Cross them out on the score sheet and add them to the other column. A scoreboard is provided for you. Each time someone lands on your property, he must pay you the number of points indicated in the top right-hand corner. Each time you land on your own property, you receive twice the points shown.

Winning Sets: Dreams (world peace, cure cancer, extend life and happy family); bedrooms (quilt, pillow, mirror and rocking chair); famous structures (Eiffel Tower, Leaning Tower of Pisa, Great Sphinx and Seattle's Space Needle)

Player One's Properties/Score	Player Two's Properties/Score

Game Card Property Pieces

On this page are the twelve game pieces for *Ben's Dream*. Cut them out and place them on oaktag to prolong their usability. Place a little box next to the gameboard as a storage area. Each time someone lands on an appropriate board space, he receives points and one of the game cards to verify property ownership. It also makes property trading much easier. The next time you play the game, design your own game card property pieces. Design a gameboard and create your own educational board game. Pick a theme. Then try to add important facts and intellectual flavor to your game.

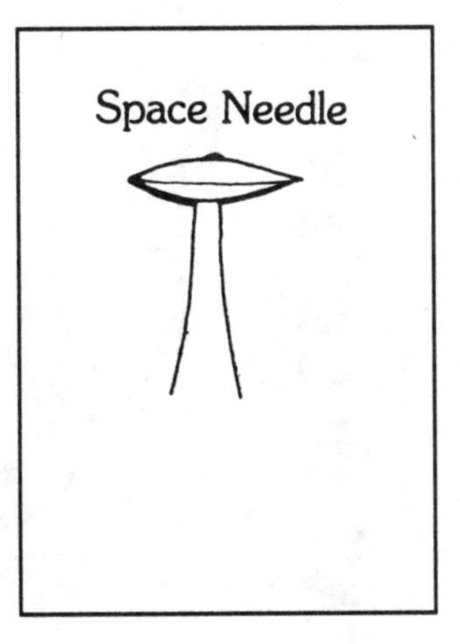

Wishes Taking You Places

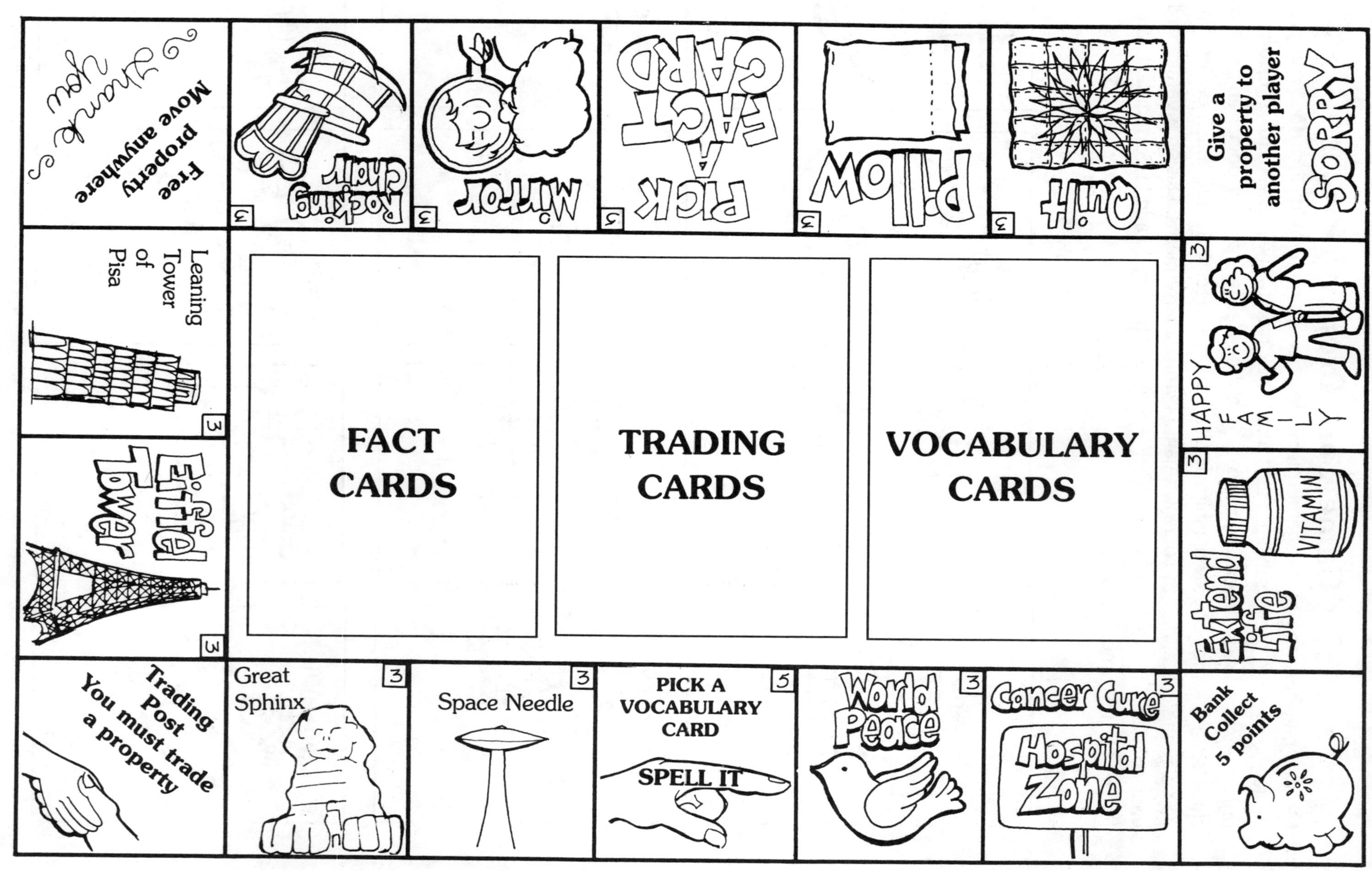

Strange Journey

A Lost Bell

First Gift of Christmas

The Polar Express

Mystery Train

Reindeer Excitement

Keep the Spirit

Joyous Children

Santa's City

Lead-Ins to Literature

What would happen if an express train stopped on your front lawn, a place where there were no railroad tracks the last time you looked, and a conductor said, "All aboard"? Of course, you would ask him where the train was going, but when he said "to the North Pole," would you believe him? And what's more, would you hop on this train with a complete stranger? This is the story of such a happening, and when you open the pages, Chris Van Allsburg's illustrations and story will make you feel like you are on the *Polar Express*.

1. What do you think the train was riding on, if it arrived on a lawn that didn't have any tracks?
____

2. *The Polar Express* sounds cold and scary. What were your first impressions when you heard the title? ______________________________
____

3. Would you draw the illustrations for a story about a polar express in color or black and white? Please explain why you chose the medium that you did. Would your drawings be clear and exact or would you use a muted style? ______________________________
____

4. You are a person that doesn't believe in anything. How would you convince the child in the story not to get on the *Polar Express*? Take the opposite point of view and show why you would encourage him to hop on the train. ______________________________
____

5. List the five responsibilities or duties that you think a conductor on the *Polar Express* would have.
____
____

6. You are a doctor who takes care of people who don't believe in Santa Claus, the Tooth Fairy or fairy godmothers and godfathers. Write your three-step program for curing your patients of their disbeliefs. ______________________________
____

7. Before reading the story, predict three stops that the express might make before reaching the North Pole. If you were the engineer, why would you stop at each of these locations? ______
____
____

8. Do you think a trip to the North Pole will be a long or short trip? Why? ______________________________
____
____

9. Suppose your parents didn't want you to ride the express alone. Who would you take on the trip with you? Explain. ______________________________
____

Just the Facts

1. What words were used to describe the steam and the metal of the train that arrived on the lawn? ____________________

2. What was in the conductor's vest? ____________________

3. What did the boy put on to run out on the lawn? ____________________

4. What animals were seen in the forest? ____________________

5. The hot cocoa on the train was as thick and rich as what? ____________________

6. Candies with ____________________ centers were eaten.

7. The train seemed like a ____________________ as it ran over mountain peaks and valleys.

8. What is the Great Polar Ice Cap? ____________________

9. Where does Santa give the first gift of Christmas? ____________________

10. The children didn't see the ____________________ when they arrived at the North Pole?

11. What shape did the crowd form at the gift ceremony? ____________________

12. Why did the train stop? ____________________

13. Where did they get the silver bell? ____________________

14. It broke my ____________________ to lose the bell.

15. How did Santa sign his note? ____________________

16. How many elves were in the center of the city to see Santa give out the "first gift of Christmas"? ____________________

17. The bell always rings for whom? ____________________

18. Who was Sarah? ____________________

19. How was the bell wrapped? ____________________

20. The *Polar Express* let out a loud blast from its ____________________ and sped away.

21. What did the child find in his pocket? ____________________

22. How did the child get to the train? ____________________

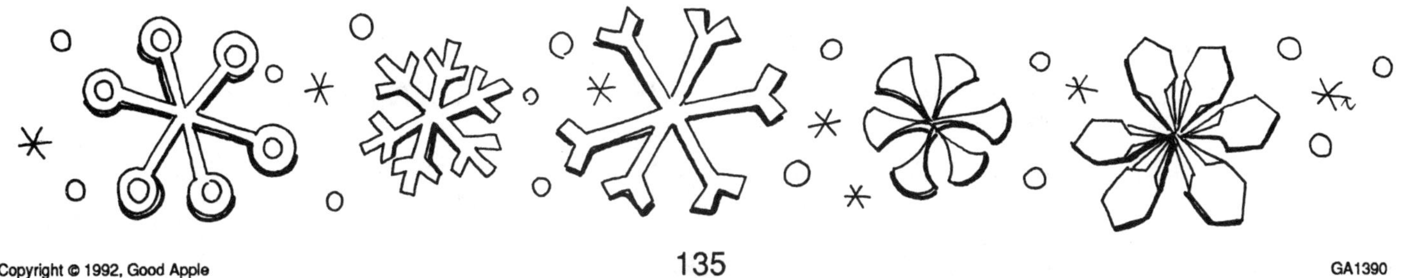

What Is Your Opinion?

1. At what age do most children stop believing in Santa Claus and the Tooth Fairy? Why do you think this happens?______

______

2. If you had a sister in the story, would you have asked the conductor if she could have come along? Don't you think the boy in the story should have brought her?______

______

______

3. Would the excitement of the trip to the North Pole have kept you from asking questions like:

   a. When are we going to get there?

   b. Why me?

   c. Where did all these children come from?

   d. How can I go out in the snow with only my pajamas on?

   Why or why not ask them? ______

______

4. What five questions should the lead character have asked the conductor before boarding the train? ______

______

5. Do you think Santa should have given the "first gift of Christmas" to more than one child?

______

______

6. The drawings of Santa Claus seem to be a little bit different than our view of what Santa Claus should look like? Why did you think the author/illustrator pictured him this way?______

______

______

7. Do you think the elves really like working for Santa Claus? What other characters would you have made helpers? ______

______

8. How would you have felt if you lost the "first gift of Christmas"? ______

______

______

9. Why do you feel that his sister no longer hears the sleigh bell's sound? Do you think the child would still hear it ringing if he hadn't met Santa Claus at the North Pole? ______

______

Vexing Vocabulary

sleigh	perfectly	polar	harness
outstretched	snowflakes	carols	knee
nougat	pajamas	roamed	approval
wolves	thundered	wilderness	lurch
scrape	peak	ice cap	silent
barren	conductor	elves	whistle

Read each sentence below. Try to record three words that mean the same thing as the underlined word in each sentence.

1. The silent hooves of Santa's reindeer tickled the roof.

   ____________________ ____________________ ____________________

2. An ice cap offers days of adventure for the daring.

   ____________________ ____________________ ____________________

3. She always wanted to be a conductor.

   ____________________ ____________________ ____________________

4. The explorers were lost in the North Pole's barren wilderness.

   ____________________ ____________________ ____________________

5. The locomotive lurched forward after being rammed.

   ____________________ ____________________ ____________________

6. Jennifer seems to look for her teacher's approval of everything she does.

   ____________________ ____________________ ____________________

7. The express thundered through the center of the city.

   ____________________ ____________________ ____________________

8. Weren't their outstretched hands a sign of peace?

   ____________________ ____________________ ____________________

9. Not even his best friend could get him out of this scrape.

   ____________________ ____________________ ____________________

10. An unknown creature roamed the countryside.

   ____________________ ____________________ ____________________

Write three sentences of your own. Underline a key word and give three additional meanings that could be substituted for the underlined word.

Sentences with Jazz and Pizazz

Drills for Skills

You will find a group of dull and uninteresting sentences below. Add three words to each sentence to give the writing some spice and zest. Below each sentence write the three words you used and grade them on a scale of 1-10 (weak-powerful) by determining how much each one helped your new sentence. Write five sentences of your own. Underline the three most powerful words in each one. Pass your sentences to a classmate and have him/her place a rating of 1-10 (weak-powerful) above each one.

Example: I lay quietly on my bed.

I often lie quietly shivering on my quiltless bed.

often 3 shivering 8 quiltless 9

1. She looked through my window.

1. ______________________________

______________ ______________ ______________

2. We travelled through the forest.

2. ______________________________

______________ ______________ ______________

3. We are gathering at Center City.

3. ______________________________

______________ ______________ ______________

4. The mountains stood above us.

4. ______________________________

______________ ______________ ______________

5. He gave us a hug and disappeared.

5. ______________________________

______________ ______________ ______________

6. The *Polar Express* sped away into the horizon.

6. ______________________________

______________ ______________ ______________

Student Sentences

1. ______________________________

Ratings ______________________________

____

2. ______________________________

Ratings ______________________________

3. ______________________________

Ratings ______________________________

4 ______________________________

Ratings ______________________________

5. ______________________________

Ratings ______________________________

Ideas and Illustrations

The six pictures below are of things that might be on the *Polar Express*. Half of each picture is drawn for you. Please complete the second half the way you think the drawing would look. Retrace the first half on another piece of paper. Then complete each picture in a completely ridiculous manner.

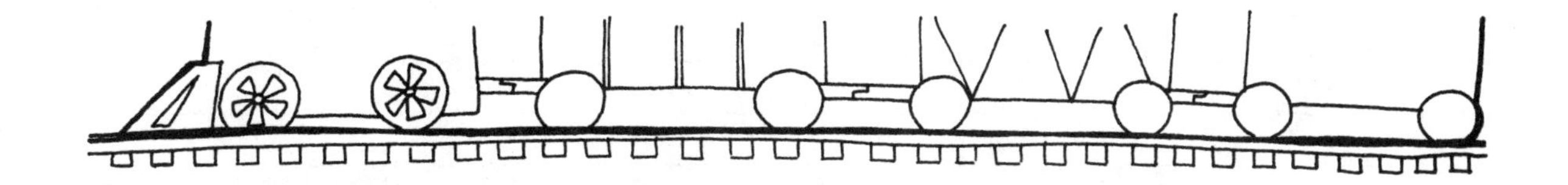

Employment Letter
Short-Term Project

You are impressed with the operation of the facilities at the North Pole and would like to become an employee of Santa's firm. You are writing a letter to him describing the job you would like to assume. Your qualifications for the position and the times you will be available should also be included in the letter. Use the space below for your first draft.

Your letter is answered by one of Santa's helpers. Use the space below to write a response to your letter the way one of Santa's helpers would write it.

You have been honored. Santa, himself, without any help from Mrs. Claus, is writing a letter back to you. Please try to design his ideas differently from the elves' style of writing in the space below.

You have been selected for a position at the North Pole. Pen a note telling Santa about your immediate arrival at the North Pole, especially if you want to be picked up by a member of the staff. Please remember that they do not take American Express at the North Pole.

North Pole Job Application Form

Short-Term Project II

You have been invited to work at the North Pole. On your arrival you have been asked to fill out the following job application form. Please answer each question to the best of your ability. Use clear descriptive sentences where possible.

First Name______________________________ Last Name________________________ M.I._____

Address Number ____

City__________________________________ State _________________Zip __________________

Age_________________________________ Grade____________________

Brother's Name ____

Sister's Name ____

Job Department (Check one or more.)

Toys _________ | Recreation_________
Children's Clothing __________ | Şick/Homeless ________
Wishes Granted __________ | Animal Husbandry _________
Post Office _________ | Letter Composition ________
Food Preparation_________ | Gift Wrap_________

Job applying for ____

Previous experience related to the job for which you are applying

____

____

____

____

____

Reason for applying for above mentioned job

____

____

____

____

Desired salary ____________________ Medical coverage_____________________________________

Lodging requirements

____

____

____

____

____

Research Suggestions

1. One of the most famous trains in the world is the *Orient Express.* What type of research items can you find about its past history and present day travels? Can you find its route, running schedule, cost and some of the intrigues that were conducted on board? Do you think Chris Van Allsburg's title was a takeoff on the *Orient Express*' name?

2. Research the four railroads that appear on the Monopoly gameboard. Do you think these were the railroads that ran into Atlantic City when the game was being designed? What other reasons can you find for their appearance on the gameboard?

3. There are present day high speed trains that travel over 240 miles per hour. What countries have these systems and would they be practical for travel here in the United States?

4. Megalevs are systems where trains are pulled along tracks by the use of a magnet's ability to attract and repel. Are there any Megalev devices in your area? How fast do Megalev system trains travel? They were supposed to revolutionize travel. What are their strong and weak points?

5. The building of the first Transcontinental Railroad, with the planting of a gold and silver spike when it was finished in Promontary Point, Utah, has hundreds of stories about it in history. What can you find out about this venture? Where are the spikes displayed?

6. Interview three members of a train crew. Focus on how their jobs interrelate for the smooth operation of the train. If you are interested in any other form of travel, you can do this for an airline crew, boat crew, hotel staff or any other group that provides a public service.

7. Call Amtrak's 1-800 number for free information about Amtrak, their trains, routes, fares and services they provide.

8. Write five humorous rules of train etiquette.

9. Pick any holiday and find three countries that celebrate it differently. Give a mini report on the uniqueness of each celebration.

10. You are the social director of the *Polar Express*. Make an imaginary *Polar Express* activities schedule for the trip to the North Pole. Schedule at least six interesting features of your day's schedule.

Teacher Suggestions

1. Have your class design the menu that might be served on the *Polar Express*.
2. We always have children design the car of the future. The same type of activity can be applied to future railway transportation. Incorporate interior and exterior design in each presentation.
3. The exploration of both poles is filled with adventurers, people with incorrect records and a host of famous explorers. Discuss why people would want to explore the North Pole, the dangers involved and the preparation that is needed for such an expedition.
4. Have your class develop the theme "Tragedies of Discovery from Ferdinand Magellan to Amelia Earhart to *Challenger 7*." The activity should focus on the mishaps and the prices we have to pay for extending knowledge.
5. Have your class fold 11" x 14" (27.94 x 35.56 cm) paper into three sections. Discuss why the child in *The Polar Express* loses the "first gift of Christmas." Would he have been more careful under the same circumstance the next time? What three circumstances would each of your students have wanted to change at home, in school or with their friends? Place an illustration above each topic and place your three ideas under each picture.
6. Set up a Chris Van Allsburg book table and design an illustration evaluation form with your class. Your students will then use this scale to rate the illustrations in each of his books. Points that can be rated might include
   a. general appearance of book
   b. creative use of shading, color and dimension
   c. uniqueness and variety of subject matter
   d. elaboration of themes and ideas
   e. coordination of story and illustrations
   f. open-ended ideas
   g. multiple interpretation of drawings

7. There is a great revival of model train collecting in the United States. Discuss the field of collecting (baseball cards; coins and stamps; designing model cars, planes, trains, villages, houses and statuettes). Make a list of the various reasons people collect and build models. Impress upon your class how important model building is to the planning and success of most industries.
8. Your local railroad yard or station will gladly host a class trip.
9. Write Steamtown U.S.A. in Scranton, Pennsylvania, for information about railroading and their historic museum.
10. Discuss the goods and services local railroads provide. Have your class list ten items found in their homes and list whether they were brought by plane, train or truck.

Write Like a Master

The theme for these story starters is the strange appearance of a train on your front lawn or in a place trains aren't usually found. They want you to look at and evaluate their work. You are sent to investigate and may treat the event in a humorous or serious manner.

Story Starter I

All right, Mr. "Wrong Way" engineer. Get this train off of my lawn. I don't care if you are picking up my little brother. This train is the world's biggest eyesore! I'll come aboard but only for a few minutes. Then I want you out of here...let me out...I'll never have the spirit. You ____________

____

____

____

Story Starter II

Do you know people who live in mobile homes, campers or on boats? I just happen to have four train cars as my home. My dad bought the land from the city and the train cars from Amtrak. The first car has our front door and leads into our living room. We took all the train seats out and put in ____

____

____

____

Story Starter III

I've been an engineer for twenty-five years and could tell you some strange stories of things that have happened on this railroad, especially this train, but nothing compares to what happened last week. It all started innocently enough as we were heading for ____________________

____

____

____

Story Starter IV

All aboard the mystery train. It will take you places and show you sights you have never seen before. Visit Again Land, where everyone has a shadow in front and behind him. Take a trip to Brainarea, where small people have big heads and big people have small heads. Visit (add three towns and ideas of your own to this train's schedule) ______________________________

____

____

____

STORY STARTER STORY STARTER

Gameboard

Materials Needed: Two number cubes, movers, light-colored crayons; Vexing Vocabulary; Just the Facts; student-made and teacher-made question cards can be placed in the areas provided for them in the center of the gameboard. They are optional but highly recommended. A card is picked each time a player has a multiple of five points in his/her bank (5, 10, 15, 20 or 25).

Players Needed: Two to four players or teams of two players

Play Procedures: Players alternate turns; throw number cubes; move in either direction at any time. This allows for playing strategies, rather than just mindlessly moving around a gameboard.

The Roll: Roll both number cubes. Your teacher will tell you to conduct some math operations with the number cubes. The three rules used most often in my classroom are

(a) Subtract the smaller from the larger; then move that many spaces (6 - 4 = 2). Move two spaces.

(b) Multiply the two cubes and move the number of spaces in the one's column of the answer (2 x 6 = 12). Move two spaces.

(c) Keep on adding the two cubes until you get one digit as the answer (6 + 6 = 12, 12 = 1 + 2 = 3). Move three spaces. Mathematicians call this finding the digital root.

Object: To score twenty-five points or to capture four good deeds, trains or forms of precipitation. Owning good deeds, trains and precipitation can be accomplished by landing on them in a normal turn, trading for them when you land on a trading post or buying one of them for two times their value when you land on the bank. Each time you land on a property you color in (or initial) the little block in the corner of the property and put the points in your running bank. Ownership will change after trades only. Cross them out on the score sheet and add them to the other column. A scoreboard is provided for you. Each time someone lands on your property, he must pay you the number of points indicated in the top right-hand corner. Each time you land on your own property, your receive twice the points shown.

Winning Sets: Trains (*Orient Express, Washington Shuttle, Denver Flyer* and the *John Henry*); deeds (clothes to poor, shelter to homeless, food to hungry and hospital volunteer); precipitation (rain, snow, sleet and hail)

Player One's Properties/Score	Player Two's Properties/Score

Game Card Property Pieces

On this page are the twelve game pieces for *The Polar Express.* Cut them out and place them on oaktag to prolong their usability. Place a little box next to the gameboard as a storage area. Each time someone lands on an appropriate board space, he receives points and one of the game cards to verify property ownership. It also makes property trading much easier. The next time you play the game, design your own game card property pieces. Design a gameboard and create your own educational board game. Pick a theme. Then try to add important facts and intellectual flavor to your game.

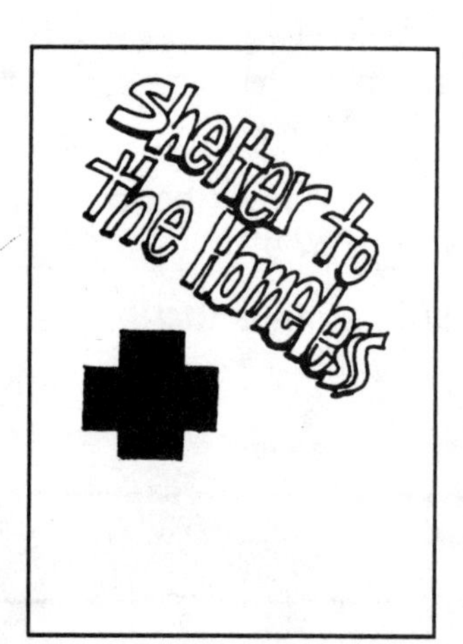

A Train of Good Deeds

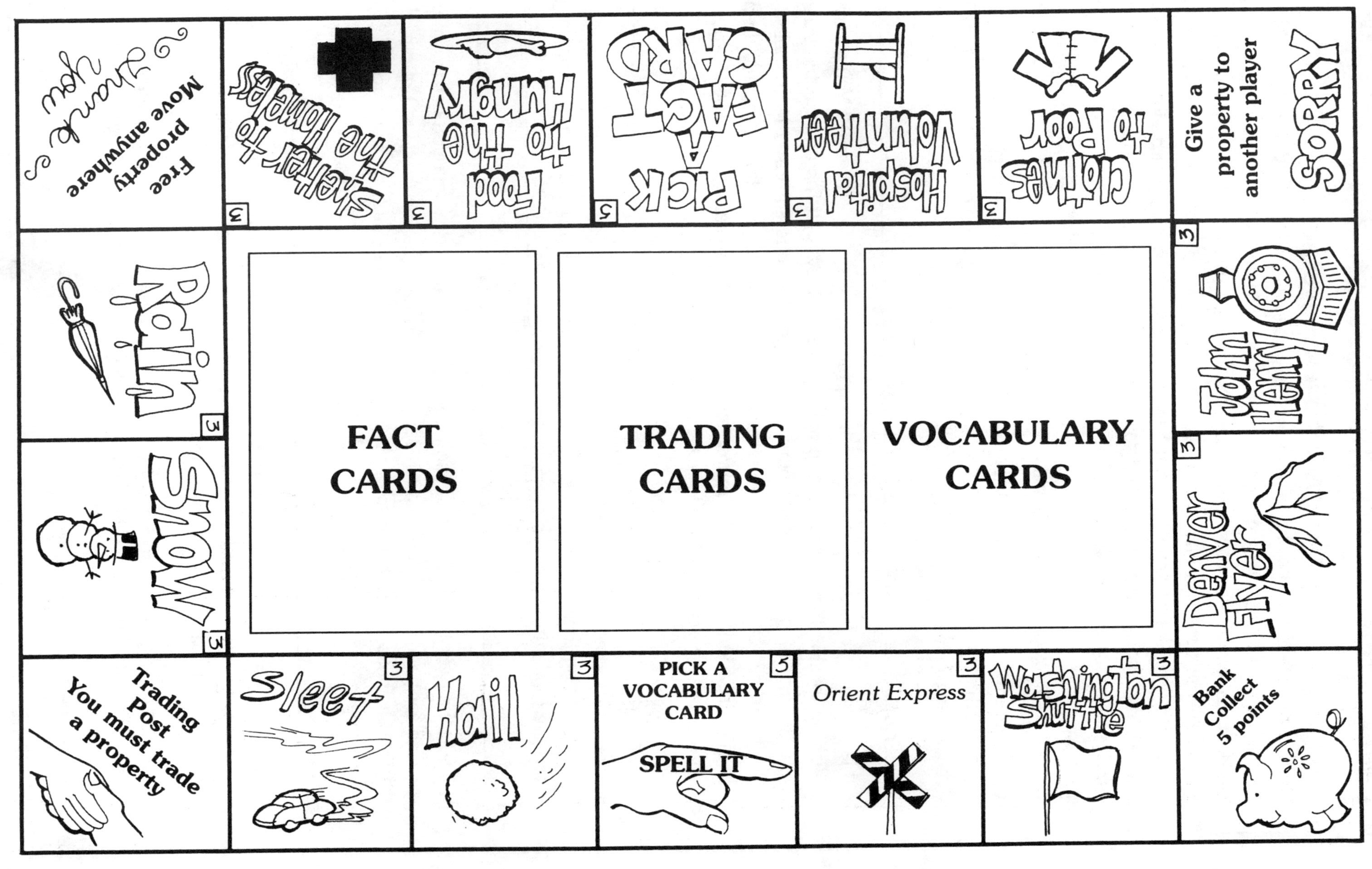

Write Like a Master

Additional Suggestions

Here are fifty additional story, writing and idea follow-ups to the "Write Like a Master" sections in each of the Van Allsburg stories that you have just completed. They should give you a wealth of additional writing formats. These formats are designed to broaden and improve your writing skills. You may continue the starters below or use them as a spin-off for your own ideas. For instance, if you don't like our theater write-up (suggestion #1), you might do a new record, TV show or new book write-up. Follow your teacher's writing assignment directions and clear your new ideas with him/her before taking off on your own. Make your selection. Then try to write additional lines for each starter on this side of the paper. Turn the paper over to continue your thoughts. Develop one new thought a week.

1. *Cats* is like no theater production that you have ever seen before. The music, story, staging and costumes will delight you. You will be on the edge of your seat rooting for your favorite cat to be reborn. One second you will be ______________________; then you will be ______________ as ______________________________.

2. Have you ever floated in the ocean in an inner tube or life preserver? You always seem to be waiting for the unexpected to grab at your feet. I knew that the unexpected was going to get me this morning! I just knew! Sure I was frightened and surprised to be pulled through my bedroom mirror to the eviler's ninth dimension. But knowing that a friendly, in need of help, hand yanked me through the mirror took some of the initial shock away. "Why me," I asked, as my mission was explained to me. I've never ______________________________.

3. I always wanted to be a nurse, but the children's terminal ward was destroying me. I know I am lessening their pain, but each suffering child seems to be draining something from me. I see the look on the parents' faces and wonder ______________________________.

4. Tooth Fairy my foot! You look like a rag picker to me. How did you get into my bedroom? I called for your help? When was this supposed to have happened? Just get out of here before I call the police. Don't give me any of that hocus pocus stuff on your way out, either. No, I don't need ______________________________.

5. Hero or goat, which is it going to be? The bases are loaded. The count is 3 and 2. It is the last of the ninth inning and immortality is staring me right in the face. I know I am going to be getting a fast ball, but should I go for the long ball or ______________________?

6. The old ballet slippers gave my feet and body a tingling sensation. Dizziness seemed to be followed by a floating feeling. Flashes of blinding light shot before my eyes as ______________________________.

7. "Backstage with ________________" (star's name) is what my article will be called. I had better bring a camera, otherwise, no one will believe my "up close and personal" interview. What should I wear? Should I put on my ________________?

8. The plague of Zendora killed thousands of Remonias, but their spirit and will to fight on was not broken. The taste of freedom is hard to remove from the mouths of the oppressed. Queen Zendora was fashioning an even more heinous plan than the plague. She was about to launch ________________

________________.

9. In 1570 Von Luber moved to Prague. His artistic talents were immediately recognized as hundreds tried to commission him to paint their wives, husbands and children. His style was a cross between ________________.

10. Sherlock Holmes is real. My great aunt Mavis worked with him on the case of the "Illusive Scorpion." At least, that is what she told the family for years. The case concerned ________

________________.

11. I always wondered what it would be like to be one of Robin Hood's merry men/women and roam the woods of Sherwood Forest in search of my companion's next meal. I wouldn't be much for sword fighting, jousting or storming castles, but I am sure my skills of ________

____

would add to the quality of life in Robin's camp. My days would be spent ________________

________________.

12. The ducks playfully swam in the pond unaware of the approaching danger. Little Ben, who was supposed to be the lookout, was busy fooling with ________________ instead of doing his job. It was too late by the time they saw the ________________

________________.

13. What was that! I don't know, but it was sure something fast. You don't think it was the Flash, do you? Not unless he can chew through six feet of cement. Handling him was as easy as passing a hot knife through butter. He fell for the old ________________

____

routine. It wasn't even a challenge to ________________.

14. Look! I do not want to see you any more. Just hang out with your friends on the weekend, because you never seem to have any time for me. I am not going to sit around wondering what you are doing. I'll find someone who will ________________.

15. Space Station Zebra calling base. We seem to have picked up some kind of interference on our transmitters. The sunspots seem to be playing havoc with all our TV monitors, also. Now what is happening ________________?

16. My mother keeps dragging me from one Junior Miss Pageant to another. I am tired of being on stage every weekend. I just want to lead a normal life. How many times am I going to have to sing "My Way" in the next year? My mother keeps telling me that I am special, but aren't all kids special to their mothers? I miss my friends and ____________________.

17. Josh, the dog, has been missing for two days. His food hasn't been touched. The last time we saw him was when he chased Mrs. Bennett's cat up the tree in her yard. I hope that nothing ____

____.

18. "Ten Days on a Life Raft" is going to make an award-winning article. If my lips weren't so parched, I could almost laugh. I'll never make it off this raft to tell my story. I was stupid to take the boat out alone. Without warning ____________________.

19. The cave's mysteries were hidden for one hundred years. All that pirate treasure nonsense that we have been hearing for years will be laid to rest, once and for all. Help me lower myself into the cavern. Hold that rope tightly ____________________.

20. I design toy cars. I am nine now and have been working on models since I was four years old. The neat thing about my cars is that they are very easy to make and even easier to paint and run. I get my ideas for designs from ____________________.

21. My mother has watched *The Wizard of Oz* over one hundred times. She says she likes it so much that she could watch it another hundred times. My dad wants to buy the tape for her birthday. If that happens, I'll never be able to use our television and VCR again. My favorite movie is ____________________. But I'd never

____.

22. Everyone in school talks about their weird dreams. All my dreams are just plain old normal dreams. They usually start with ____________________.

23. The fire raged out of control. Thousands of acres of forest land were being destroyed. The loss of animal life was devastating. The shifting winds were bringing the blazing inferno closer to town. Our water supply ____________________.

24. The hopscotch champ of America is ready to begin her final approach. She picks up her favorite throwing stone which she calls "Blue Velvet," because of its deep-blue color. As the wind blew her wavy hair into her face, she began her quest for her third straight title. It would not be easy this year, because last year's runner-up ____________________.

25. Has anyone written the book *Stuck to My Braces*? If it hasn't been written, I certainly have some unbelievable chapters for such a book. Bubble gum, the rug and my sister's hair will be some of the less interesting chapters. The more interesting ones will include __________

____.

26. Help me move this desk, please. There is something shiny under it. Look! It's moving. Hold my legs and pull me out if I yell to you. What kind of friend are you? What do you mean, you'll run if you hear me scream? I need your ____

____

27. All my spare time is spent working on kites. My dad gave me part of his workspace in the garage. I made this kite by myself. It is a cross between a ________________________ and a ______________________________. I got the idea from ________________. It is a magazine that loads of people use for creative ideas.

28. Next to stepping into puddles and eating mud, my little brother doesn't do much of anything. He always ____.

29. We have tried every type of treatment for your son, Mrs. Johnson. What we need is some kind of miracle to find the correct antidote. The rash has disappeared, but he still has not come out of his coma. We are thinking of trying ________________________________.

30. We haven't seen land in thirty days. The men are about to mutiny. "Crow's nest watch, do you see anything?" He can't hear me in all that wind. My eyes are even playing tricks on me. I thought I saw a bird. It ____.

31. A horse's life is a good one. We are one of the best cared for animals on the farm. The food is good. The barn is warm. The back rubs are frequent. Wait a minute. Why am I saying things I don't believe? Being free to run the hillside is better than this. Not that I am ungrateful. It's just that no one should give up his freedom for food, comfort or __________

____.

32. Jump into the water. It is fantastic. Cherry Jell-O isn't as smooth or enjoyable. No, that's not it. How am I going to advertise the benefits of coming to our beach? How about this approach. Mix sun, sand and water for ____.

33. I can't get out of bed on Monday mornings. My body just wasn't made to leave my bed for school on Mondays. We kids should boycott Monday mornings. Then we could spend the time ____.

34. The painter's brush strokes weaved a tale of ____.

35. Have you ever been splurred? It almost defies description. It is one of those feelings that you'll never forget. It slowly starts at your toes working its way up your body until it slams into your brain. It was perfected by the Zenonites on the planet Voltar. The weapon ______

____.

36. I wonder what is in my lunch today. Yesterday a little rabbit was eating the lettuce in my ham and cheese sandwich. Two days ago a jellyfish was swimming in the milk next to my peanut butter and jelly sandwich. Last week a miniature baseball player was sliding into the chocolate of my Baby Ruth bar. I knew it! Look at that ______________________.

37. The storm doesn't look like it is going to let up. There doesn't seem to be any way for me to contact home or get off of this island. The rain caught us completely by surprise. Even if our rowboat hadn't broken away from its moorings, it is much too dangerous to be out on the lake. Jim's idea of ____

____.

38. I enjoyed the sea snake article that Rasheed presented. Even sharks are afraid of the sea snake. It is one of fifty varieties of aquatic snakes found throughout the world. Ramon's sea creature presentation was on ____.

39. I miss the band and their support. My manager said the club could afford only a solo. The engagement has been going well. Tonight I go solo with my first original song. The melody of the song is easy to sing. My troubles are with ______________________________.

40. Hypnosis can be very dangerous in the hands of the untrained. Martha thought reading one book would make her an expert. As soon as she put John to sleep and couldn't get him out of the trance, we knew she was no expert. When John started screaming in his trance ____

____.

41. After playing the computer simulation "Life and Death," I felt like I was William Harvey teaching a class on the circulation of blood in the year 1615. The simulation taught us about operations, medical procedures and ______________________________.

42. Play, magic harp, play. You worked for that ugly old giant. Now it is my turn. I don't know any Jack. Just do what I tell you. If you don't ______________________________.

43. Look, Little Red Riding Hood, do I look like the type of creature that is going to cause you any harm? Of course not. I would like to help you carry that bag to Grandma's house. When we get to the stream, you can get on my back and I'll carry you across. You can wrap your arms around my neck so you don't get wet. Grandma and I are ______________

____.

44. The scarecrow moved. Yesterday it was in the middle of the field. Today it is in the back corner. No, I haven't been reading ghost stories or the "Twilight Zone" mysteries. No, there isn't any full moon tonight. Sure, Halloween is just around the corner, but why would I want to scare you and myself at the same time. It just doesn't make any ______________

____.

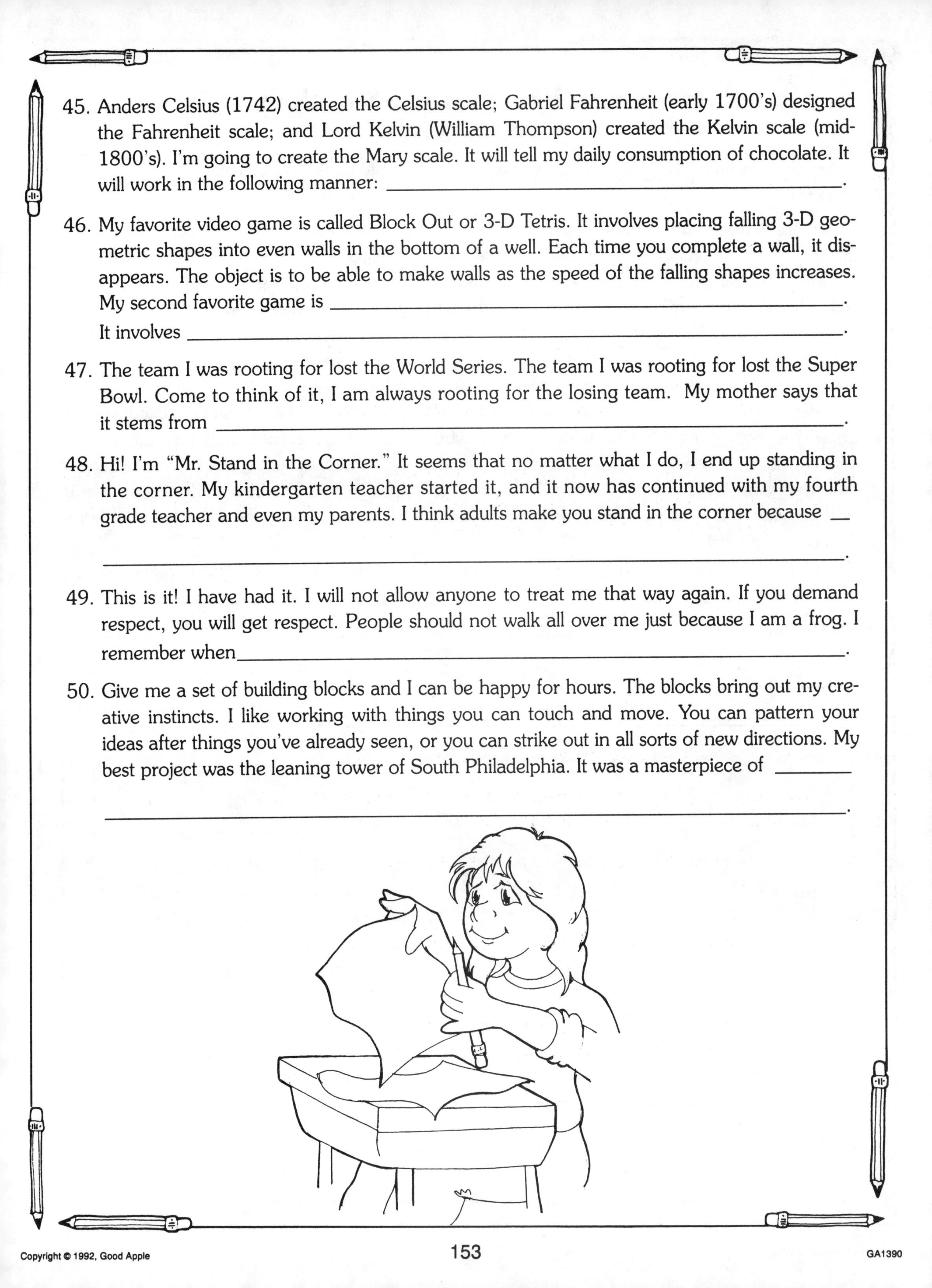

45. Anders Celsius (1742) created the Celsius scale; Gabriel Fahrenheit (early 1700's) designed the Fahrenheit scale; and Lord Kelvin (William Thompson) created the Kelvin scale (mid-1800's). I'm going to create the Mary scale. It will tell my daily consumption of chocolate. It will work in the following manner: ______________________________.

46. My favorite video game is called Block Out or 3-D Tetris. It involves placing falling 3-D geometric shapes into even walls in the bottom of a well. Each time you complete a wall, it disappears. The object is to be able to make walls as the speed of the falling shapes increases. My second favorite game is ______________________________. It involves ______________________________.

47. The team I was rooting for lost the World Series. The team I was rooting for lost the Super Bowl. Come to think of it, I am always rooting for the losing team. My mother says that it stems from ______________________________.

48. Hi! I'm "Mr. Stand in the Corner." It seems that no matter what I do, I end up standing in the corner. My kindergarten teacher started it, and it now has continued with my fourth grade teacher and even my parents. I think adults make you stand in the corner because __ ______________________________.

49. This is it! I have had it. I will not allow anyone to treat me that way again. If you demand respect, you will get respect. People should not walk all over me just because I am a frog. I remember when______________________________.

50. Give me a set of building blocks and I can be happy for hours. The blocks bring out my creative instincts. I like working with things you can touch and move. You can pattern your ideas after things you've already seen, or you can strike out in all sorts of new directions. My best project was the leaning tower of South Philadelphia. It was a masterpiece of ________ ______________________________.

Ideas and Illustrations Supplement

Bulletin Boards

Dear cartographers, architects, sign painters, teachers, students and bulletin board makers of America,

There are twelve pages in this section. Each page represents a month of the year. The page is divided into two parts. The upper section contains an idea for a classroom or hall bulletin board for the particular month indicated. Teachers might want to take a piece of transparency paper, trace the bulletin board idea, put it on an overhead projector and outline the enlarged image the projector creates. The lower section is a bulletin board that has been started, but needs student help to complete. Students are asked to give their input as to the direction additional writing and illustration should take. Please complete the student bulletin board with your original and humorous ideas. A monthly clothesline of student bulletin boards makes a great display. A blank bulletin board has been provided below for students who would like to create a bulletin board from scratch. Students can use this blank board to create ideas for their other subjects as well. Transfer your best ideas to 11" x 14" (27.94 x 35.56 cm) art paper and pin the best work of the class up in the hallway. Try having a bulletin board contest after your teacher gives you a general theme for your original work.

Student name____

My bulletin board theme is ____________________________________.

Bulletin Board Idea for September

Fill Up with September's Ideas

Color and complete the bulletin board idea below.

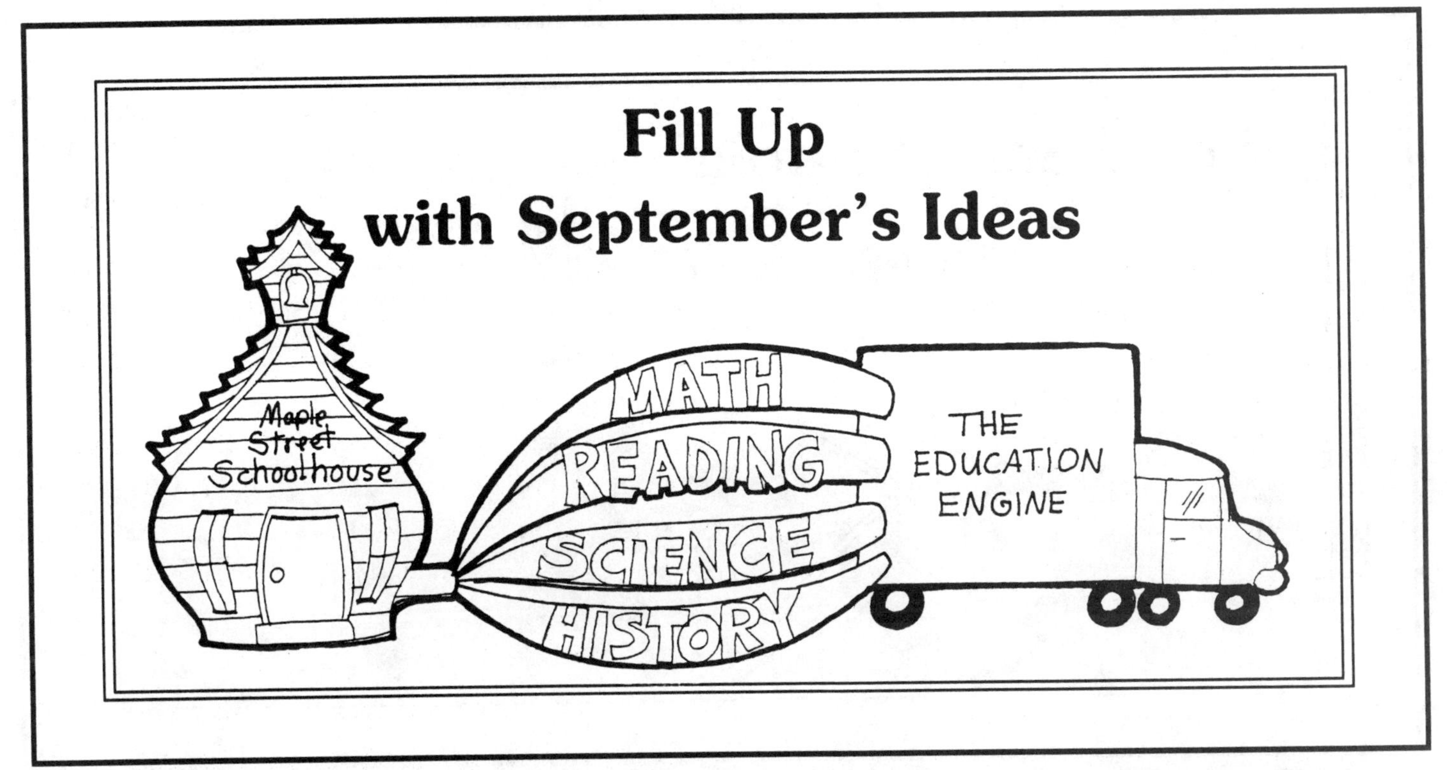

Student-Generated Bulletin Board Idea for September

Enjoy September's Science

Color and finish the bulletin board idea below.

Student: Add five of your own ideas to this bulletin board.

Bulletin Board Idea for October

World Series Books

Color and complete the bulletin board idea below.

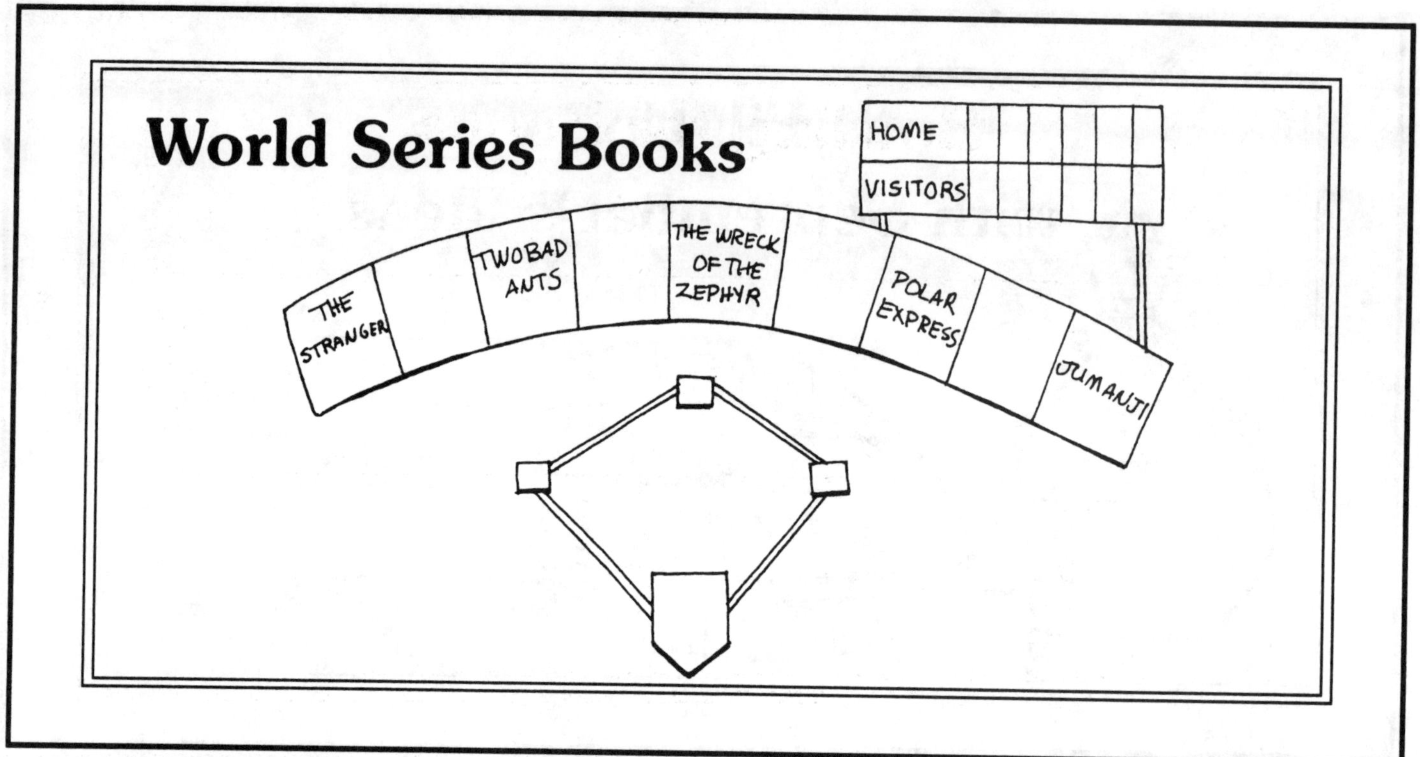

Student-Generated Bulletin Board Idea for October

Mind-Biting Books

Color and finish the bulletin board idea below.

Student: Draw some additional Halloween creatures that read.

Bulletin Board Idea for November

Bowling for Books

Color and complete the bulletin board idea below.

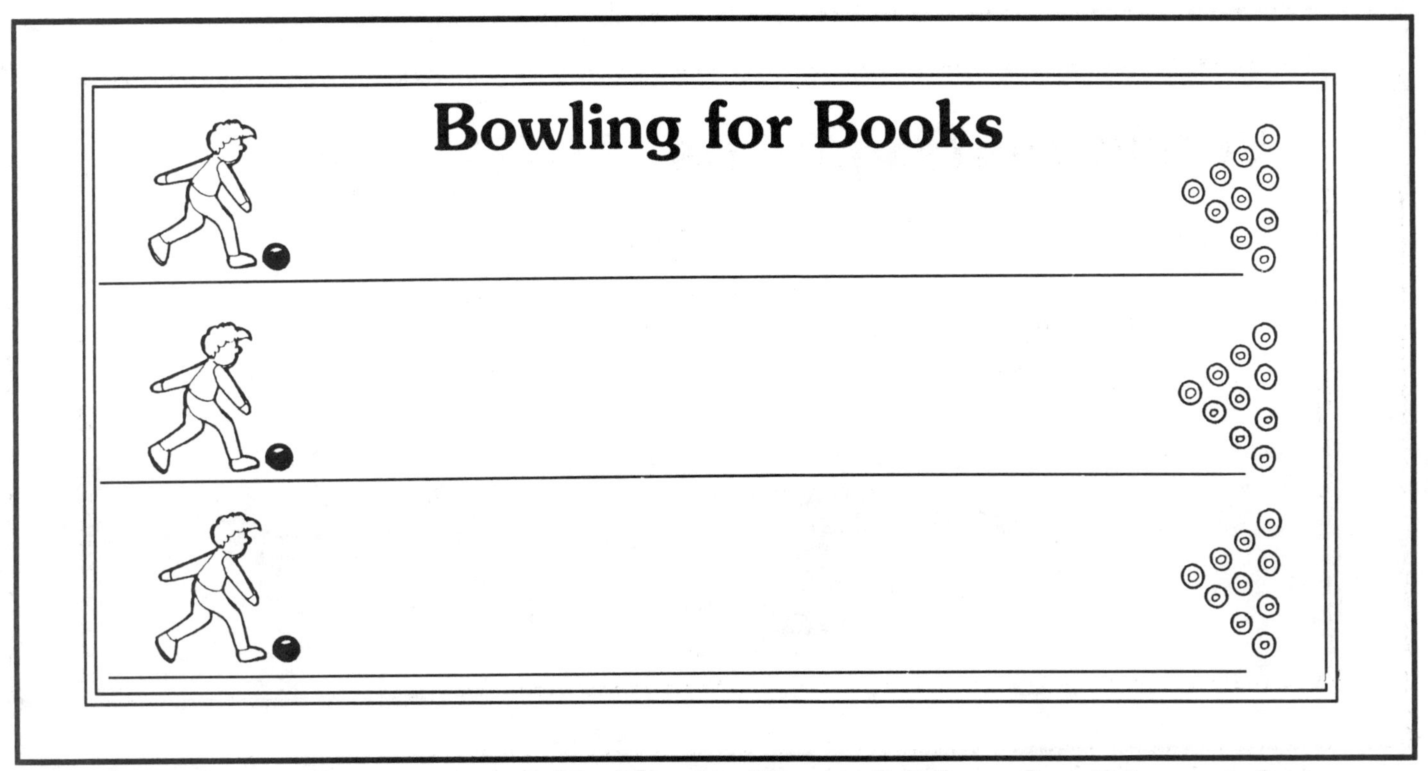

Student-Generated Bulletin Board Idea for November

Even the Headless Horseman Reads

Color and finish the bulletin board idea below.

Student: Draw other characters from literature who love reading.

Bulletin Board Idea for December

Presenting Chris Van Allsburg

Color and complete the bulletin board idea below.

Student-Generated Bulletin Board Idea for December

The Wonders of Winter

Color and finish the bulletin board idea below.

Student: Draw illustrations for four ideas that you would consider winter wonders.

Bulletin Board Idea for January

The Super Bowl of Books

Color and complete the bulletin board idea below.

Student-Generated Bulletin Board Idea for January

New Year Delights

Color and finish the bulletin board idea below.

Student: Add three ideas that would be a new year delight for you.

Bulletin Board Idea for February

Books Are Filled with "Love"ly Ideas

Color and complete the bulletin board idea below.

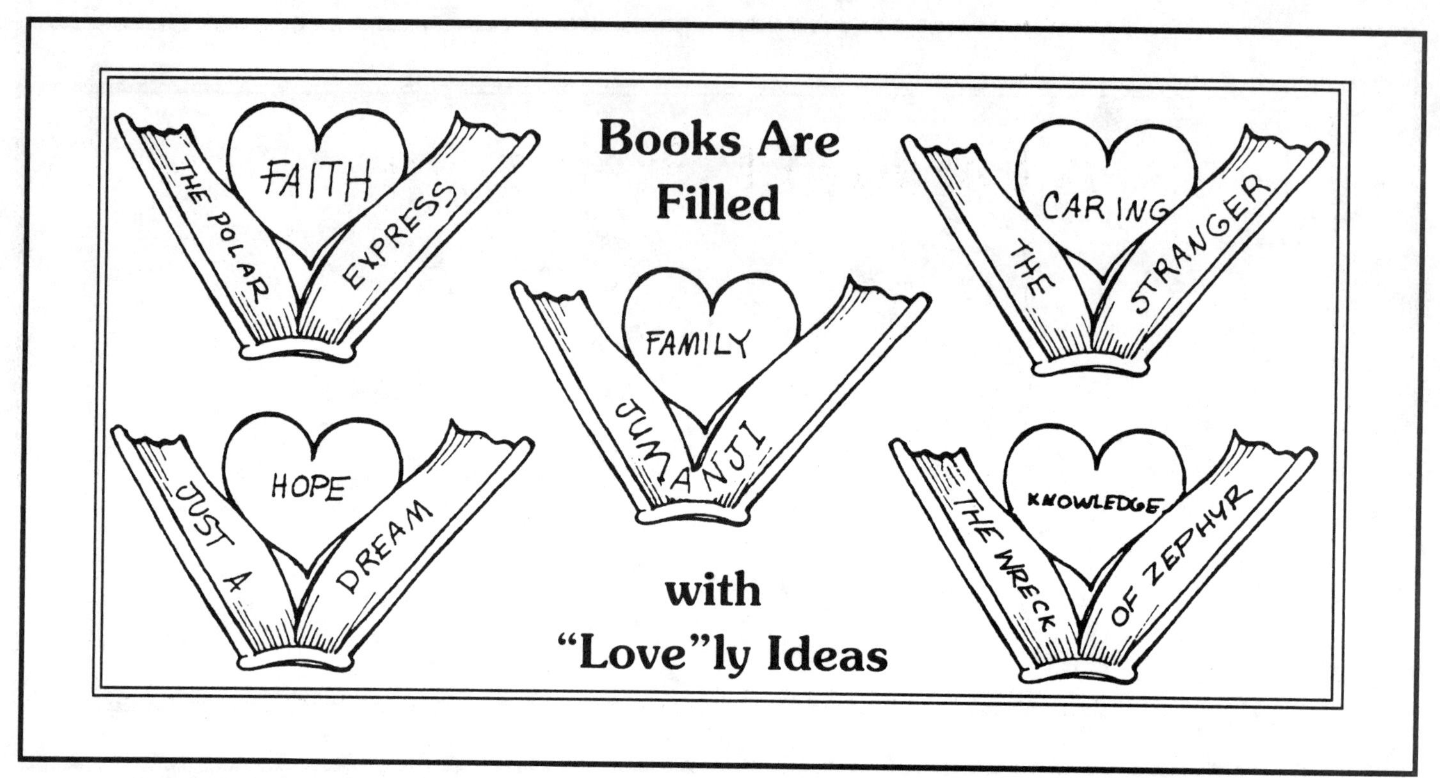

Student-Generated Bulletin Board Idea for February

Heartbreaking Books

Color and finish the bulletin board idea below.

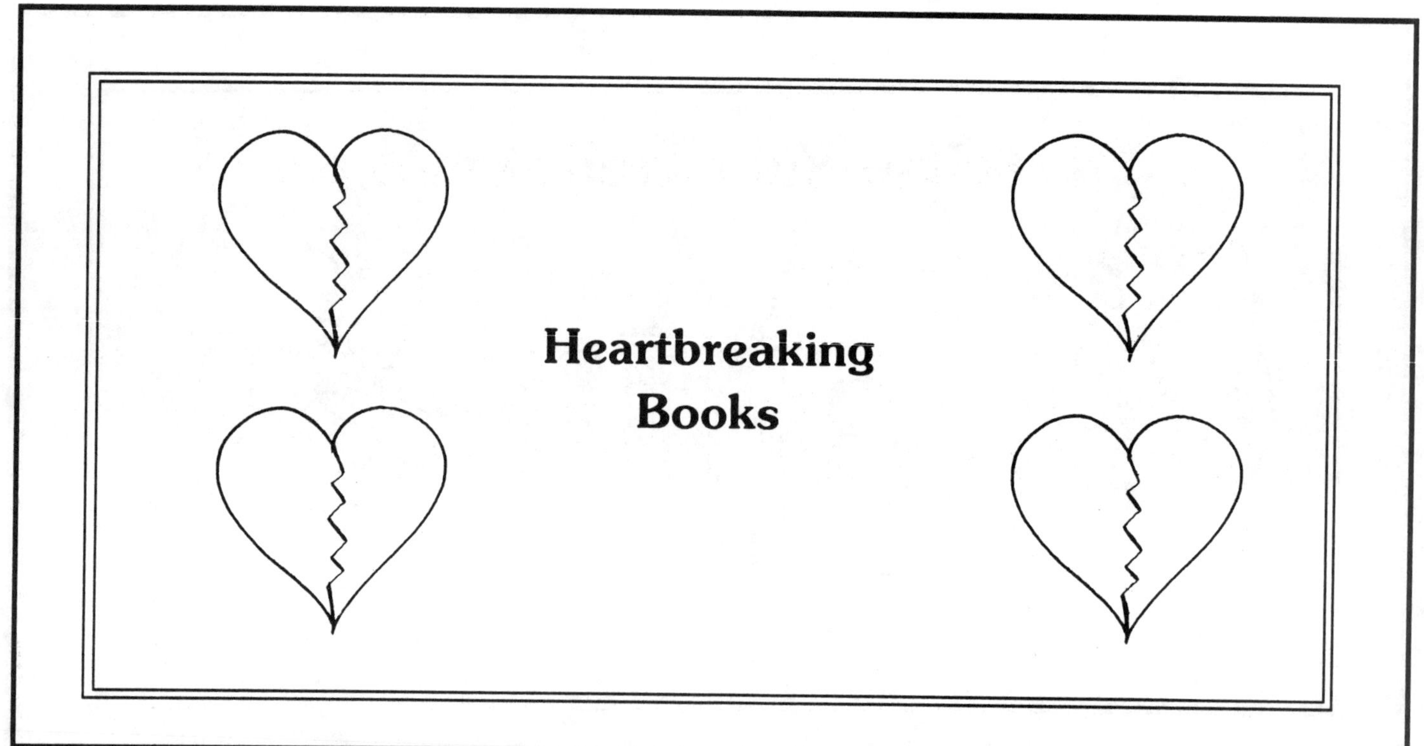

Student: Add six "tearjerkers" to this collection of books.

Bulletin Board Idea for March

A Parade of Great Books

Color and complete the bulletin board idea below.

Student-Generated Bulletin Board Idea for March

These Books Are Knockouts

Color and finish the bulletin board idea below.

Student: Draw four books and an illustration next to each that might give an idea about the book's story.

Bulletin Board Idea for April

Stepping into Literature Favorites

Color and complete the bulletin board idea below.

Student-Generated Bulletin Board Idea for April

Ideas "Spring" from Books

Color and finish the bulletin board idea below.

Student: Draw five books and light bulbs with ideas you know "spring" from books and reading.

Bulletin Board Idea for May

"May"be Literature Is the Key

Color and complete the bulletin board idea below.

Student-Generated Bulletin Board Idea for May

"May" the Gates to Excellence Be Opened by Books

Color and finish the bulletin board idea below.

Student: Place three book titles and illustrations to the excellence area.

Bulletin Board Idea for June

Good Books Keep Your Mind Afloat

Color and complete the bulletin board idea below.

Student-Generated Bulletin Board Idea for June

Summer's Songs

Color and finish the bulletin board idea below.

Student: Draw three of your summer reading books and their illustrations below the selections above.

Bulletin Board Idea for July

Feed a Book to Your Mind

Color and complete the bulletin board idea below.

Student-Generated Bulletin Board Idea for July

Summer Sizzlers

Color and finish the bulletin board idea below.

Student: Draw four books and their illustrations. Select titles that would make good pool, beach or lake reading.

Bulletin Board Idea for August

Dive into These Books

Color and complete the bulletin board idea below.

Student-Generated Bulletin Board Idea for August

August Eye Openers

Color and finish the bulletin board idea below.

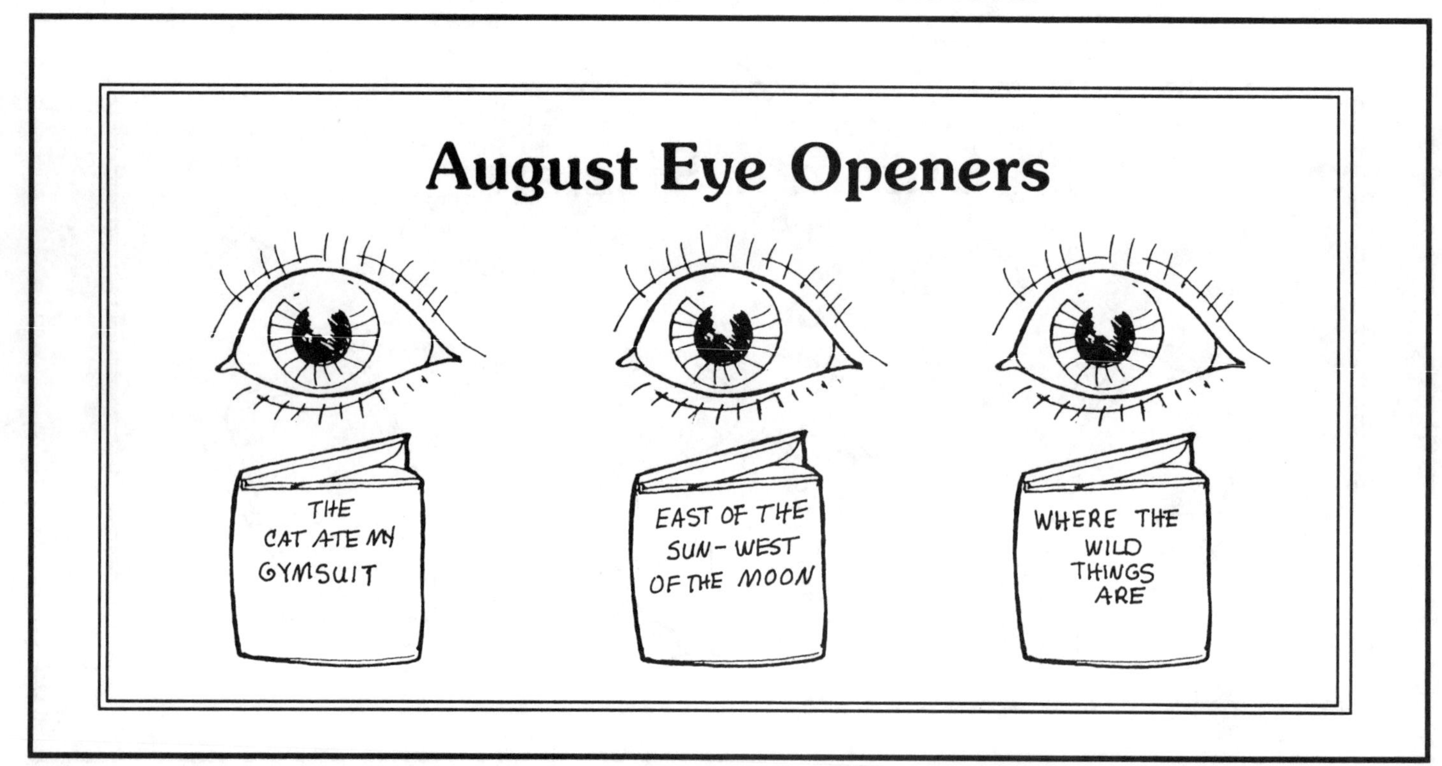

Student: Draw five books that you would consider August eye openers. Place an illustration next to each one.

Answer Key

Just the Facts, page 3

1. the opera
2. a jungle adventure
3. very important
4. chair
5. seven
6. a dozen
7. heavy rains
8. guide
9. a herd of rhino
10. a python
11. the mantel clock
12. the monkeys
13. fireplace
14. jumanji
15. under a tree in the park
16. Danny Budwing
17. sleeping sickness
18. a tray of food
19. puzzles
20. instructions
21. one turn

Vexing Vocabulary, page 5

1. fawn yawn
2. centipede stampede
3. dozens of cousins
4. winter splinter
5. Drano volcano
6. meek, shriek
7. bored ignored
8. noon monsoon
9. bizarre car
10. gone python
11. fair square
12. muzzle puzzle

Just the Facts, page 18

1. 3, lightning
2. a cane
3. the bottom
4. bones
5. a rabbit
6. a dog or wolf
7. a bowl
8. too large for the stage
9. Answers will vary.
10. Answers will vary.
11. Answers will vary.
12. H, stripes
13. 5, rabbit, dog, fish, bird, human
14. ice, ice cream, frozen yogurt, plastic, etc.
15. nails

Just the Facts, page 32

1. Bailey
2. He seemed never to get tired.
3. country road
4. his memory
5. See you next year.
6. fall
7. local doctor
8. leaf
9. out of place
10. Everything had changed colors except the farm.
11. animals
12. deer or other animal

Vexing Vocabulary, page 34

1. shy
2. loner
3. sometimes
4. breeze
5. banged
6. fall
7. shook
8. amazed
9. living room
10. draw

Strange Word, page 35

1. range
2. rag
3. garter
4. Grant
5. ranger
6. Stan
7. anger
8. star
9. rats
10. rare
11. gnat
12. rear
13. tag
14. ant
15. gears
16. stare
17. earn
18. rate
19. great

Just the Facts, page 46

1. Peter Wenders' home
2. thirty
3. PW's children's/friend's stories
4. tiny
5. five
6. a boomerang
7. two weeks
8. man, lamp, table
9. the fog
10. one
11. a turning doorknob
12. the fifth chair
13. vines
14. by a country stream
15. Maple Street
16. three
17. caterpillars
18. fall, Halloween, Thanksgiving
19. caterpillars
20. a bird
21. Venice

Vexing Vocabulary, page 48

1. Menace—Venice
2. pal–canal
3. bought–thought
4. width–fifth
5. giggle–wiggle
6. thunder–wonder
7. rated–fascinated
8. tight–downright
9. dessert–desert
10. intern–lantern

What's in a Name? page 50

2. shark
3. ski
4. Raid
5. arid/Arrid
6. bird
7. iris
8. brush
9. chair
10. hard
11. kid
12. radish
13. rabid

Just the Facts, page 62

1. a scout ant
2. the queen
3. long and dangerous
4. spiders
5. ants' antennae
6. smells, wind, sky
7. glassy
8. nervous
9. fell asleep
10. silver
11. boiling, brown
12. a whirlpool
13. cave
14. temperature
15. rocket
16. toast
17. a waterfall
18. half eaten
19. strange

Anthill Revisited, page 65

1. can't 3/4
2. antiques 4/8 =1/2
3. anteater 4/8 = 1/2
4. plant 4/5
5. lantern 5/7
6. Santa 3/5
7. antifreeze 5/10 = 1/2
8. antelope 4/8 = 1/2
9. Atlantic 5/8
10. anthem 4/6 = 2/3
11. Grant 4/5
12. pants 4/5
13. Planters 6/8 = 3/4
14. canteen 4/7
15. want 3/4
16. Santa Fe 4/7
17. tantrum 5/7
18. giant 3/5
19. chant 4/5
20. Atlantis 5/8

Just the Facts, page 76

1. Fritz
2. Miss Hester
3. furniture, pillows
4. his hat, to keep the dog from eating it
5. retired
6. Abdul's house
7. bell
8. Abdul Gasazi
9. dig up flowers, chew on trees
10. fresh dog prints
11. tears
12. in magic
13. had been captured
14. absolutely, positively
15. tremendous

A Flower by What Name Did You Say? page 79

1. carnation
2. rose
3. tulips
4. hemlock
5. daisy
6. marigold
7. lilac
8. dandelion
9. iris
10. pansy
11. sunflower
12. poppy
13. snapdragon
14. gladiolus
15. petunia
16. daffodil
17. crocus
18. violet

Just the Facts, page 91

1. Rose
2. television
3. in a huge dump
4. jelly
5. Floral Avenue
6. toothpicks
7. on the woodcutters' jackets
8. throat, eyes
9. medicine
10. Hotel Everest
11. two
12. Coffee, a phone
13. the Grand Canyon
14. the ducks
15. motor
16. tree, yo-yo, dinosaur, gun
17. Rose's great, great grandson

Drills for Skills, page 94

1. valley/alley
2. steam/stem
3. stand/Stan
4. free/fee
5. arid/rid
6. seven/even
7. match/math
8. crash/rash
9. glove/love
10. store/sore
11. split/spit
12. fairy/fair
13. plants/pants
14. open/pen
15. tank/tan

Just the Facts, page 106

1. a pipe
2. by a storm
3. find a breeze
4. ominous
5. a sea gull
6. wind
7. head
8. They were sailing above the water.
9. stranded on land away from water
10. tide
11. treacherous
12. strangers
13. incorrect sails
14. oyster
15. Samuel Blue
16. stars
17. church spire
18. shifting winds
19. odd jobs
20. a cane

On and Off Words, page 109

1. cotton 2/6 = 1/3
2. coffin 2/6 = 1/3
3. ton 1/3
4. offense 3/7
5. King Kong 2/8 = 1/4
6. doff 1/4
7. office 3/6 = 1/2
8. Stone 2/5
9. offspring 2/9
10. sonic 2/5
11. offside 3/7
12. Oregon 3/6 = 1/2
13. toffee 3/6 = 1/2
14. tone 2/4 = 1/2
15. wagon 2/5
16. offend 2/6 = 1/3
17. scoff 1/5
18. don't 1/4

Just the Facts, page 121

1. shopping
2. black
3. baseball
4. the next day
5. tape
6. Father's easy chair
7. drumming
8. rocking house
9. Statue of Liberty
10. 1:30
11. buoy/marker
12. sea gulls
13. George Washington
14. mitt, baseball time
15. Great Sphinx, porches
16. half
17. gravel driveway
18. Mount Rushmore
19. Washington, Jefferson, T. Roosevelt, Lincoln
20. geography book, rain
21. her jaw

Just the Facts, page 135

1. hissing, squeaking
2. a pocket watch
3. his slippers and robe
4. wolves, rabbits
5. melted chocolate bars
6. nougat
7. roller coaster
8. a barren desert of ice
9. center of city
10. elves
11. circle
12. It could go no further.
13. reindeer's harness
14. heart
15. Mr. C
16. hundreds
17. those who truly believe
18. the boy's sister
19. in a small box
20. whistle
21. a hole
22. Santa's sleigh